Imagination

Imagination
Embracing a Theology of Wonder

CHERYL FORBES

MULTNOMAH · PRESS

Portland, Oregon 97266

Cover design and illustration: Britt Taylor Collins
Edited by: Liz Heaney

IMAGINATION
© 1986 by Cheryl Forbes
Published by Multnomah Press
Portland, Oregon 97266

Printed in the United States of America

Library of Congress Cataloging-in-Publication Data

Forbes, Cheryl.
  Imagination: embracing a theology of wonder.

  Includes bibliographical references and index.
  1. Imagination—Religious aspects—Christianity.
I. Title.
BR115.I6F67   1986   233'.5   86-811
ISBN 0-88070-136-6

86 87 88 89 90 91 92 – 10 9 8 7 6 5 4 3 2 1

To My Mother,

Who Lives Imagination Every Day

Contents

Chapter 1

The Cracked Ring

Years ago, Madeleine L'Engle told me that Jesus was not a theologian but a God who told stories. In a book on imagination, God, the *imago Dei*, and worship, it's appropriate to begin with a tale. Or a tale within a tale; it's one story in this world and quite a different one in another . . . maybe. So, let me tell you a story.

Once upon a time there lived a little boy and his sister, who was much older than he was. They lived in a big house with other members of their family, but when they played together, it was just the two of them as though nobody else existed. Of all the games they played, the one the little boy loved best was "story."

"Tell me about the man in the ring," he would say.

The ring in question was a man's black onyx with the silhouette of a knight embedded in it, a kind of inverted cameo. The other interesting feature about the ring was that it had a crack right through the middle of the man's face. It was a Mary Poppins ring because every few months or few days, just when need was greatest and boredom at its highest for this little boy, the man in the ring would leave the ring and go off on a mighty adventure, cracked helmet and all.

The little boy had wonderful times watching the adventures of his fractured knight through his mind's eye. At first, though, the child had trouble seeing the knight, but every time his sister said the magic words to release the knight from ring bondage—where he had been placed by a witch—the child's vision grew brighter.

The Witch claimed to be the legitimate heir to the throne. Not many people had ever seen her. Those who had didn't know she was a witch because she was so beautiful. Anyone that beautiful, they thought, had to be as good as she looked.

Down through the years the people had been fortunate in their rulers. They had received kindness and land and plenty of food and clothing so they always expected the best from their rulers. But when the young, homely knight took over, the Knight of our tale, things began to go wrong. Crops withered, weeds flourished, bugs were large and abundant, young people refused to work or when they did, they hated it and did a bad job. All in all, the land, Dendra, was pretty topsy-turvy.

The Knight knew, of course, that he wasn't to blame for all these things. He was the only one who knew the Witch had put a twisting spell on the land. Whatever started out to be whole and good twisted on itself, becoming the opposite of what was intended at the beginning. Corn and other crops that tried to grow straight and true to the sun would suddenly bend down and around and snap in two and so wither. But part of the Witch's cunning was that she made the suffering of the land seem random and haphazard. People always hoped they would escape. Yet since it happened so regularly, no one could relax happily and live their lives as they had been taught to do. Life no longer had any predictability. That was what everyone missed the most: peace. The people had always looked to their ruler to provide peace and security, but not any longer. "If it isn't the Knight's fault," they said, "he still should be able to do something about it. He's the ruler, after all."

The poor Knight was quite befuddled as to what to do. He had good intentions, but his actions suffered under the same twisting spell as everyone else's. The difference was that he knew who was responsible—the Witch. But how to fight her? She was hard to find. For one thing, she never stayed in one place long; that was too boring. The Knight supposed that if he would resign and give her his job, she might be happier, maybe less bored, but he couldn't be sure. He had always thought that the only reason she twisted things was to see what would happen, as a child might destroy a toy to see if he liked it better that way. He thought and thought, but, no, he couldn't just give her the whole country to play with. Who knew what she would do then?

When all this twisting business first started, he rode out every day to look for her. "Just talk some sense into her," his old granny insisted. "Or," she added menacingly, "if that doesn't work, box her ears." But how could he do either unless he could find her?

Some days he got close. He knew because suddenly his horse would twist around and head back the way he came. And Gumples was a most obedient horse. Gumples' owner knew the Witch was twisting him around. It really exasperated the Knight, but no matter how his court wise men experimented, they could find no antidote to her spell. So nearly every day he would hop on Gumples and, with a few of his best friends from the castle, head out east, north, or south. The Knight knew she would never be west of the castle. Although the West was the most beautiful area, you had to travel through some pretty thick brambles to find the gardens and blue-white springs and natural fountains. He knew that the Witch would never find the beauty because of the brambles. So, he never rode west. That was one of the things that bothered him most. He loved riding to the West. Now he couldn't go there any more.

What he didn't know, though, and the Witch had discovered quite by accident—she would never have thought of it on her own—was that if you went east long enough you could get into the West by a back door that had no brambles at its entrance. The Witch was big on getting things the easy way. She hated to work for things or spend too much time figuring things out. If she couldn't do it first off, she probably never would. If she hadn't taken to witching immediately, who knows what she would have become. Nothing else would have been as easy. Of course she only knew the simple spells, but since it was more than anybody else in the country knew, she was a success.

So all the time the Knight was looking for the Witch to the east, north, or south, the Witch was living in the West, on the other side of the brambles. The Knight was a kindly and well-intentioned ruler, but when it came to figuring things out, he was no better than the Witch. In that they were well-matched. After trying for so long to find her and never succeeding, a smarter (though perhaps less kindly) man would have begun to suspect that somehow the Witch had moved west of the castle. But accidents can happen to knights as well as to witches. He found her one day, lounging beside a fountain, dressed in royal purple with a witch-designed tiara on her lovely head.

She had long ago given up wearing ragged gowns with tattered sleeves and patches at the elbow. Nor was she one of those witches who believed that ugliness was part of the persona of witching. She wasn't exceptionally bright, it's true, but she knew that people responded better to a prettily dressed and well-scrubbed appearance. A beak nose and a wart with three hairs just didn't seem becoming in a witch—no matter what all the old stories said or what the pictures of other witches showed. She had turned her mousy brown hair into a rich auburn, straightened her nose so that it just turned up a little at the tip, smoothed out her skin, and uncrossed her eyes. (Well, to be truthful, the last spell hadn't worked quite so well as she had hoped. Her eyes were still slightly crossed, but you got used to that.)

That's what she looked like when he found her. Actually, Gumples found her. The horse was tired to death of riding in vain, so he insisted—brambles notwithstanding and obedience-training cast aside—on heading west. When he and his knight reached the fountain, the Knight at first had no idea he had found what he'd been seeking for so long. The Witch didn't fit any of his notions of witchiness. That was his first big mistake, and of course that was what the Witch wanted since that was how she'd managed to spread dissension and dissatisfaction among the people in the first place. She simply looked too good not to be trusted.

And the Knight did trust her. He began to make some gallant speeches, using all the courtly phrases he'd been taught as a boy. She enjoyed listening to him talk, but she knew that he didn't recognize her. Now, in this one way the Witch played fair. She wanted her enemy to know who she was—that is if he ever had the fortune to find her. She'd decided that a long time ago. Well, now he'd found her. (Actually, she'd let him when she didn't turn Gumples around.)

In the middle of one of his best speeches—something about her eyes, I think it was (she was still a little touchy that she hadn't got her eyes quite right and hated to be reminded of them)—she said, "Don't you want to know my name?" Which was, of course, the one thing it hadn't occurred to the Knight to ask. He wasn't too sure he even knew his own name; everyone always called him the Knight. And then, of course, there was the great responsibility of knowing another's name. What if he lost it? Or forgot it? Or said it wrong? Or worse yet, spelled it wrong? There could be serious consequences for the other person should he mislay the name somewhere.

He thought about it awhile. Finally, he said to the Witch, "No, I don't think I care to know your name just now, thank you. Maybe some other time."

But she could tell him *what* she was, which was really another way of asking what she did. People usually addressed others by what they did—the Knight or the Farrier or the Smithy or the Cook, the Butcher's Wife, the Park Planning Commissioner, the Agro-bureaucrat, whatever. (It really got confusing if a town had more than one butcher or carpenter; names would have been much simpler, but even with names there are only so many to go around.)

"I'm the Witch," she said.

At first he wouldn't believe her. Reluctantly, however, after she turned Gumples from a gelding to a zebra and back again, the Knight had to admit that she probably was the Witch, and why hadn't she said so in the first place so he needn't have made a fool of himself with all those courtly but flirtatious speeches. She laughed. Not a tinkling or throaty or hearty laugh, but a true witch's cackle (she couldn't find any spells to change it). With that, she sent him into the ring only to be released every seven years to look for her, or whenever someone said the magic words. She didn't want life to get too dull.

And so I became acquainted with the story of the man in the ring, a story the little boy loved to hear, a story he could see with his third eye as clearly as he could see the entrapped knight in the ring. He saw with his mind's eye. He heard with his mind's ear. He smelled and touched with his mind's nose and fingertips. He used his imagination.

The little boy never asked what the story meant or why things were the way they were. He accepted them because he believed them. He probably knew with a part of him that no man in a cracked, black onyx ring could come to life. But that didn't make the adventure less real or the possibility of adventure less exciting. He understood that the Witch was wicked and that wicked people exist and that they don't always look the way you think they will. He knew that good people exist and that they aren't always smart just because they are good. He also knew that accidents happen and you learn things without ever having to figure them out. And he knew the importance of names.

No one taught the little boy these things, but nevertheless he knew them; his young imagination told him that all this was so.

As people get older they listen less and less with their imagination. Instead they listen to facts or reason or what can be observed in the physical world. But facts can lie, and reason can become sophistry. What we observe in the physical world may not be all there is to the universe, as physicists in quantum mechanics have discovered and continue to discover. Although imagination can lead us away from the truth as well as lead us toward it, the potential for understanding truth is always greater when perceived with imagination. The great scientists, composers, painters, and ordinary people whose lives express equilibrium and peace in the face of triumph as well as tragedy have never neglected their imaginations. They can still sit, as that little boy, and see that there is more to life than meets the physical eye.

Our third eye, the eye of imagination, needs to be open and clear to see God, to know him, to worship him, and to accept the world he has given us. That's what this book is all about.

As for the Knight and the Witch and the cracked ring, they're always ready when we need them. They may return.

Chapter 2

Dispensing with Creativity

S ince nineteenth-century Romanticism became the cultural norm, we have been in love with *creativity*—always pronounced in italics. We urge our children to be creative and spend a lot of money to make certain they have every opportunity to be so. We take up the hobby of creativity as adults, as if it were counted cross-stitch or softball. We read books on creativity or take courses on how to improve creativity. Corporations offer seminars to make their managers more creative. Managers respond by telling people to "get creative" during meetings or in their jobs. Creativity, now big business.

Yet no one really knows what creativity is or where it comes from. We probably mean "originality" when we say "creativity." Being original was not a priority from the times of the Greeks to the nineteenth century. It shouldn't be now, but it is. Most of us suspect that we don't have much of either creativity or originality, but we won't admit it because people disparage the uncreative. (It's ironic that what often passes for creativity is merely bad art or bad craft. This happens because imagination is left out.)

Most people assume that when we talk about imagination, we really mean creativity. Not so. That, too, is a holdover from

17

the nineteenth century. Every person has an imagination; not all of us have creativity, which is only a function of imagination. Creativity results in art; the result of imagination might be art, but it could just as easily be something practical.

When we think of people with imagination, the names of Einstein, Bohr, Bettleheim, or Lloyd Wright might come to mind. Or any number of composers, musicians, painters, sculptors, and researchers. But never our own name or our neighbor's or our spouse's or our boss's. If asked, we would probably say that none of the people we know has any imagination. Yet we might call these same people creative if we know that they have interesting hobbies (or any hobbies at all other than watching television or reading *Time* magazine).

These people do have an imagination. So do you; so do I. Whether or not you or I exercise it—and most of us don't—is another question. Most of us don't use our imagination because we don't know God has given it to us; nor have we been taught how to use it. Despite the ballyhoo about creativity, our educational system, for the most part, fails to show people how to use imagination. Churches certainly don't emphasize imagination, nor do businesses. In fact, all of society has stripped imagination from us and replaced it with a false notion of creativity.

Again, creativity and imagination are not the same. Each of us has imagination; we need to resist the notion that only certain segments of society have and can use it. Imagination need not result in what civilization would call creativity, art, or invention, although it may be necessary for any of those activities. Imagination is also necessary for ordinary living.

Imagination, the *Imago Dei* Within Us

Let me put it in theological terms. Imagination is the *imago Dei* in us. It marks us as God's human creatures. It helps us know God, receive his grace, worship him, and see life through his eyes. That means, imagination is a way of seeing life—or ways of seeing life. Throughout the rest of this book I try to show imagination at work from as many angles as possible, which is really the only way to understand imagination. As C. S. Lewis put it, imagination is "the organ of meaning." All the information we receive about God, our responsibility as his stewards, our roles as husbands, wives, sons, daughters, siblings, employers, or employees are so much dust without imagination to help us act on the information. Imagination is, to borrow a phrase from the Book of Common Prayer, our means of grace and our hope of glory. It humanizes us in the truest meaning of that word—by making us more like Christ, the only completely imaginative person who ever lived.

Jesus' life has been studied, compartmentalized, and scrutinized in every way but the way he lived imaginatively. No one has looked at his life merely to see how he used his imagination. His commandments can only be kept using strong and supple imaginations. Paul, too, writes of the demands of the Christian faith, which, if taken literally, would force us to enter the nearest monastic community. Even then, with the removal of many of the daily tasks that make up ordinary living, we would still not become reasonable, whole, and living sacrifices without using our imaginations. It's a matter of changing our way of seeing. Most of us muddle along in predictable patterns. What imagination helps us see is that any life, no matter how ordinary, is extraordinary with God. He shattered ordinariness with the Incarnation. We just haven't got the message yet.

Stopped-Up Sinks

Many Christians long to live unencumbered for God, fulfilling every commandment, praying ceaselessly, worshiping without reservation. But then the trash starts to accumulate. Or the dirty dishes stack up. Or the sink stops up, the grass gets out of hand, and the baby smells like ammonia and an outhouse combined. Not to mention the matter of earning a living to put food on the table so there will be garbage to empty to provide trashmen livings to put food on their tables . . . and on and on. Ordinary life. Is it any wonder that our churches are filled with frustrated Christians who are barely able to keep up with worship attendance and whose bones audibly crack at a request to teach Sunday School or befriend a newly divorced man and his children?

We *know* we cannot give any more of ourselves. We know we cannot act out in any more meaningful way what it means to be a Christian. And we *know* that we are not fulfilling our foremost responsibility—worshiping the Creator from whom we have life at all (and garbage to empty and gardens to weed). We don't know how. We don't know what it means. Even if we did, there is little time and no energy left to concentrate on worship, even on Sunday mornings. So we struggle along, getting farther and farther away from our reason for having life to begin with.

Western theology, particularly since the Reformation, has emphasized propositions, a particular way of knowing truth that discounts imagination in favor of reason. We need to correct the imbalance in our lives and somehow find for ourselves what we weren't given in school or church. We need to seize imagination.

Ripping Up the Recipes

Our Christian faith and life is a mystery. We cannot begin to understand or logically explain why God chose to favor a sinful people with his Son or why he gave us his Spirit to lead us into his kingdom. We cannot adequately describe the exchange of the Eucharist. Unlike medieval men and women, we are uncomfortable with mystery. Abstractions disturb us. That which is unseen makes us queasy and distrustful. We want to quantify our lives so they can be easily explained and understood. Forty hours of work, eight hours of sleep, two hundred church members enrolled, forty people saved a week, ten days of vacation, and so forth. Some of that is necessary to maintain structure to life. The existence of time is the primary structuring principle we have, much more important to us than space, for example. But constantly quantifying life leads to predictability. It allows us to presume a certain amount of scientific control over our existences, even though at one level we know that life is not a matter of correctly mixing various ingredients to give us the perfect Viennese torte. Life just isn't a collection of recipes.

Unfortunately, we've disregarded the truth that God works in mysterious ways his wonders to perform. We'd rather he didn't. We could do with a little less imagination on God's part so that we didn't feel so overwhelmed by our own lack of it.

We cannot completely return to the Middle Ages, where women and men saw life alive with image and metaphor, where the music of the spheres existed and could be heard by the ears of imagination, and the dance of the stars could be seen with the eyes of imagination. The Renaissance, the Industrial Revolution, and high tech society have sufficiently destroyed any residual attachments we might have had with those days. We have "de-imaged" our lives. (Some would blame this on science, yet thanks to science, imagination is back in the discussion. For example, there are mysteries that cannot be summarized neatly and propositionally in the study of quantum mechanics, where two particles in the subatomic world seem to be in two places simultaneously.)

Our reliance on propositions and our desire to quantify have stripped life of imagination, but so also has our compulsion for making life easy or boredom-free. If society has stripped imagination from us, it wasn't that difficult to gain our participation. We have participated almost willingly. The evidence surrounds us. When children no longer know how to play, can no longer make up games or think up "let's pretend"— and there is a new generation for whom this is the most difficult task that could be asked of it—when adults find little pleasure or interest in conversation, whimsy, or nonsense, then we have reached the stage where imagination means nothing to us. So why should we care that we aren't taught what it is or how to use it? Of course, we don't realize that what we are trying to avoid— namely, boredom—is the inevitable result of no imagination. Entertainment gadgets are no substitute for an ever-expanding imagination. With an active, fertile imagination, loneliness could be a stranger and angst an ancient disease. TV and the dinners it spawned may be a lucrative business, but they deprive people of more than just vitamins.

So we must shoulder some of the burden for our lack of imagination. We have offered it up as Faust once offered his soul—not realizing what it was, why we had it, or what to do with it, and thus certain we could live without it. Faust had an advantage over us: he knew he needed to recover his soul. Do we realize how crucial it is for us to recover imagination?

Life would be easier without imagination, with no faculty for sensitivity, perception, instinct, memory, or a way of participating in that which is greater than ourselves. Most of us at some point have felt that we would be happier without emotions (of course a contradiction in itself; without emotions we would be neither happy nor sad). As any honest Christian would admit, it also would be much easier not to have aligned himself with the triune God, such are the demands he makes. Yet, how much less does life mean without imagination.

Christians have been settling for mediocrity in every aspect of their lives. Whether from frustration or exhaustion is unimportant. It was too late for Faust to recover his soul; it is not too late for Christians to recover imagination. We can tarnish the *imago Dei*, we can ignore it, misunderstand it, misuse it, barter with it, or block it up. We can also figure out what it means and go from there.

Chapter 3

"Use Your Imagination"

How many times have we heard someone say, "Use your imagination"? How many times have we urged this on our children or parents? This common command really means, "Think. Go beyond yourself. Put yourself in another sphere. Transpose yourself into a different situation. Understand what I'm saying intuitively. Use your common sense." We mean all that—and probably more—by those three words, "Use your imagination." It assumes that we and those to whom we direct the command know what imagination is and how to use it.

What does the phrase "use your imagination" tell us?

First, "use" implies that imagination can be exercised. Imagination is more than intuition, which comes and goes as it pleases and is outside our control. We have something in us that we can call on to "imagine." Some people may equate imagination with reason; others see it as a separate faculty of the intellect or as a bridge between reason and intuition. I have called it the *imago Dei* in us. However we define it, it's obvious we agree we can do something with it.

The next word in the phrase is "your." This assumes that a person actually does have an imagination. We've all had times when we look at someone in amazement and exclaim, "Don't

23

you have any imagination?" We've also known children and adults who lack the ability to make believe. They may be uncomfortable without mental barriers or with time and space to fill: nothing prescribed, nothing predetermined, no set schedule, activity, or event. These people frequently find themselves bored, always longing to be entertained or informed. They are passive creatures with inactive imaginations. Despite appearances, such people do have imagination, but for some reason they have never learned the right exercises to use it.

Finally, we have the word "imagination" itself. "Use it," we plead with people; it doesn't occur to us that people don't *really* know what we're talking about. But a person can't use his imagination unless he knows what are the works of imagination—image, metaphor, symbol. We need to understand all of these.

Much of what we think of as imagination is an outgrowth of Kant or Hume and such nineteenth-century poets as Shelley and Coleridge. In this century psychologists, psycholinguists, and educators have each contributed their views. Although many of these people have approached imagination as the vehicle through which creativity comes, others, such as Sartre, have attempted to study imagination itself. A few theologians have thought about imagination as it relates to understanding the nature and will of God—that is, the role of imagination in propositions. Few Western theologians have considered imagination as the means to worship. Eastern orthodoxy comes much closer to a theology of imagination, if I may so term it. The Eastern view of worship, metaphor, and image demands that imagination play a central role in interpreting Christianity. But before we look closer at some major approaches to imagination, we must look at the object of imagination, the image.

The Importance of Images

In Protestantism, as in Judaism, the idea of an image is similar to the idea of an idol. The command not to engrave any images or to have images of any kind that could become objects of worship is deeply embedded in our consciences. Yet, we can have images without worshiping them if we recognize that an image, whether it be a concept or an object, is merely a symbolic representation of a reality beyond and above us. Life would be next to impossible without images and their relatives, symbol and metaphor. The mystery in life, the joy of creation, and the means for celebration and worship itself would be lost without images.

Look at some common and not so common images. The first and strongest is the image of the Last Supper or the Eucharist. We reenact the Lord's final Passover with his disciples when we celebrate communion. They, of course, were reenacting part of the ancient history of the Israelites. This image (as do all images) provides continuity, context, and a connection from generation to generation. It is no accident that this celebration focuses on a meal—the homeliest, most necessary act of living. Our meal, the Eucharist, uses the basic elements of life—bread and wine, food and drink. These are images of Christ's body and blood. His initial sacrifice for us and our participation in it during communion—our taking the images in all their profundity—foreshadows the celestial banquet.

We know that the Lord's Supper is an image. The cross, too, is an image to which people respond intensely (some of those responses are maudlin, others quite legitimate). Jewish people, too, respond emotionally to the cross. For them it stands for the seas of shed Jewish blood throughout the centuries. Chaim Potok in *My Name Is Asher Lev* deals with this profoundly. Ultimately, the young, brilliant painter Asher Lev can find no images in his own image-bereft life to express the anguish and beauty of sacrifice, and he is forced to turn to the cross. He can find no greater expression of physical agony than in the crucifixion paintings of the masters. People need images, whether they are artists like Asher Lev or you and I trying to understand the Christian life today. For many Christians, the deep image of the cross has connected them to the root of their faith.

Although the Eucharist and the cross, either empty or with Christ still in place, are the two main images of Christianity there are many others. The empty garden tomb is one. First-century Christians used the image of a fish, which some people still display today on car bumpers and leather handbags. The dove represents the Holy Spirit; a servant or a steward is an image for an entire segment of Christian theology.

Ours is an image-rich faith. If we are not conscious of the images that mark or define our Christianity, we lose a primary way God communicates his truth to us. It also becomes difficult to understand the work of imagination, which is to *make* images. Without images our memories would be empty (for memory is "nothing" but a series of images), our lives bereft of meaning. Too, without image-awareness, we are easy victims of images that influence our thinking often without our realizing it, images antithetical to our faith.

Despite our ignorance of them, images surround us; we cannot function without them. What would we do without stop signs, for example? Or a flag on a country mailbox? Those are simple, ordinary examples. Susanne K. Langer would call these signs, not images; she doesn't deal with images in *Philosophy in a New Key*. But we live with images that we no longer realize *are* images. Money, for example, represents value or goods and services. Clocks and watches are images of something we call time. (Try defining time; it's impossible. No one knows what it is, but we certainly know how to measure it.) The development of clocks and watches has changed society.

The alphabet is a collection of images that represent sounds in our language. When we use the alphabet to form words, which are themselves images, we are making physical something that is essentially mental. Words, phrases, sentences, paragraphs, pages, and so forth, merely symbolize ideas or meaning. It is our primary way of communicating. Using images, no matter what they are, no matter how sophisticated or simple, means communication. Without them, we cannot understand each other or clarify, even to ourselves, how we understand our world.

Dorothy L. Sayers would say that using imagination reflects the mind of our maker, the first and only person to imagine anything without the aid of memory or prior experience. Although it probably smacks of Neoplatonism, I see the world— trees, stars, grass, horses, water—as images and aspects of God's mind. For example, a tree is an image of God's strength and justice, a daisy represents his playfulness and love. I don't pretend I can know what God had in mind when he created nettles or nightshade or cosmos; I'm sorry for the weeds and thrilled by the flowers. Nor do I particularly want nightcrawlers anywhere in my vicinity, but when I'm out for catfish or perch, I'm glad they're around (and that I've learned not to scream and squirm when I'm hooking them).

But just because I don't understand it all, doesn't mean that somebody else doesn't have a clearer idea than I. I'm grateful for poets, songwriters, essayists, novelists, and yes, at times even advertisers, who see images in every red holly berry or through every blade of grass. At the very least I can participate in their vision through the image and gift of the language we hold in common. George Orwell's image of a pig farm and its connection to politics or Garrison Keillor's small midwestern town stretches the sinew of my imagination and makes me conscious of those images that crowd my life. Before I know it, I see images everywhere. I haven't brought them into existence; they've been in front of me all along, but my imagination lacked sight and smell. Those insistent jabs encourage me to wake up.

Recognizing Images

Each of us should be able to bring images to mind; each of us does so daily. The images may be nostalgic or bittersweet. They may be contained in a memory or be part of a task. An image may bring to mind a picture or a scene. Another may be more connected to a smell or a feeling. These symbolic representations can come from anywhere and be made of almost anything. The important thing is to realize that you and I have images in our lives. Certain images may have become your favorites over the years. A stone wall is an image of privacy for a New Englander or an object of beauty for someone who loves the look and feel of stonemasonry. For another, a stone fence may merely be a utilitarian image—it holds up a bank or keeps the cows in.

Children have great ability to invent images, which some people remember well into adulthood. My grandfather, who was a dairy farmer in northern Wisconsin, died when I was only five years old. When I was quite small we lived with my grandparents. I have few memories—or images—from those years. though my mother's photographs help connect me to that time. Yet, I still have an intense love and longing for my grandfather. For years I carried in my imagination the image of the two of us fishing. There stands Grandpa, so tall, lean, and strong with me next to him. We're on a bridge—high, high above a wild waterfall slapping into a river. And that's where we fished. Even though today I don't like heights, this image, full of excitement and a sense of danger, holds no fear.

For twenty years I never knew whether this image came from an actual event or a dream. I had asked my grandmother about such a bridge and waterfall; I had asked my mother. They didn't recognize it, though Grandma told me that yes, Grandpa had taken me fishing. And then, a couple of years ago we went to a place called the Chute. There it was, our fishing spot. It looked nothing at all like my image of it—it was small, tame, and not at all high—yet I recognized it instantly. When I told Grandma that this was the place I had asked about, she matter-of-factly said that Grandpa had fished here quite a bit.

To me, though, there was nothing at all matter-of-fact about the discovery. It was rather like stumbling onto the Isle of Avalon to find Merlin still alive and Arthur about to be crowned king. On the one hand, a person would be thrilled to find that the image of Merlin and Arthur is true. On the other, he might be disappointed to find it less imposing than his image. Forever after he would carry those two conflicting images with him, as I do about the place where Grandpa and I had fished. Since the day I discovered that my image was true, I've never been quite pleased to have made the discovery. I'm not convinced that it made my image any truer to know that the place actually existed.

That is the deepest image I hold, and though it is simple and hardly profound, it has provided me not only with a good memory and comfortable, secure feelings, but also with an understanding of what ordinary, serviceable love means. I understood that Grandpa was sharing one of his great pleasures with me because he loved me. I think of the toddlers I know. I'm not sure I'd take any of them fishing. I don't recall how I behaved, but I hope I minded my fishing manners out of love and some perception of what it meant to Grandpa.

The ability of children to invent images is, for some psychologists, one of the qualities that marks childhood. Maturity is its loss, though this needn't be the case. Perhaps more than children, adults need to think in images and to recognize their significance. Today, however, children as well as adults seem to have missed the experience of images and imagination.

The Impact of Images

The work of imagination, then, is the *making of images* (and metaphors and symbols, as we shall see). Daydreaming can be an imaginative activity, as can invention and philosophy. My image of my grandfather and me fishing has philosophical as well as theological implications. My imagination produces those kinds of images. If your imagination runs more to the practical than the poetic, it doesn't mean that it functions incorrectly or that it isn't imagination at all. Many people use images to help them with daily tasks, athletes in particular.

Particularly successful collegiate swimmers, professional baseball players, or golf pros see themselves winning a race, game, or tournament before they begin. They create an image of themselves doing what it is they want to accomplish and then watch the scene with their imaginative eyes. Although some people might call this positive thinking or even wish fulfillment, it shows an active, legitimate use of imagination. These people are creating new images rather than remembering images that already exist. Neurophysiologists have discovered that the brain responds to these mental images as if the activity were actually happening. There is no difference in the brain waves whether an athlete is swinging a bat or only seeing an image of himself doing so. It's an imaginative warm-up. Whether it's an athlete's image of himself performing a skill or whether it's a crucifix, images—physiologically and metaphysically—have power.

Images are a more compelling way of understanding truth than is logic. In many instances, an image compactly explains a truth that might take several paragraphs or pages. It presents truth with an immediacy and impact lacking in other means of communication. Images are signposts, compasses, maps that aid us. They simplify yet enrich our lives. They help bring order out of chaos—or prevent chaos from occurring. Think what would happen if every time someone saw a Do Not Enter traffic sign or the double no passing lines he needed even a brief explanation of what they mean.

Our Senses and Imagination

Up until now, I've talked only of images as the work of imagination, deliberately using the concept of images in only limited ways—as visual and as intimately related to memory. These are the two most common views of imagination. Some psychologists and philosophers, who have long argued about what imagination is, link it directly to sight. An image is usually something a person envisions. Without a memory of what an object looks like, mental sight would be impossible. Imagination is inextricably linked to memory. Neurophysiologists working in the area of learning and memory have discovered that the brain has a section to handle images. Near the hippocampus is an area called the amygdala, located at the tip of the temporal lobe, which is part of the limbic system. The hippocampus functions in simple recall, but the amygdala arranges what scientists call "memory images," the work of imagination.

Although for most people the relationship of memory and sight to imagination is the best way to begin thinking about the subject, it only touches a small aspect. Do people born blind lack imagination? If imagination is the meaning of the *imago Dei*, then everyone—blind, handicapped, mentally impaired— all has imagination. People born blind may have no visual memories. For them—and even for those with sight—sounds, touch, or smells may trigger intense images more powerful than any created by sight. Again, scientists have explained in the case of smell, for example, that the olfactory fibers are directly connected to the hippocampus and the amygdala. Sight must go through several intermediate connections. For sight to be as direct a connection as smell, the brain would need to be about ten times larger than it is; we would never be able to hold up our heads, much less walk, if that were the case. Certainly, some people are moved more by sights, others by sounds or odors, while still others may find words the vehicle to explode the imagination. But if the "memory image" is connected to emotion, it is most likely stored in the amygdala.

Every type of image is possible within one person. We all know people whose imaginations are so lively that music, poetry, the scent of garlic, or the sight of swamp grass provide imaginative fodder. Obviously, it is common for people to respond more to one imaginative stimuli than another; thus we have poets, composers, painters (to me a combination of sight and smell), or potters (a combination of touch and sight). Think of the richness of Beethoven's imaginative hearing, where his memory of sounds and his ability to create new images of sound combined into such incomparable beauty. He was a genius; some people might call it an unfair example to use him in this context. Yet perhaps his greatness came not so much from his genius as from his ability to work at imagining sounds and how varying sounds related to one another.

Mozart, too, heard music in his head (all composers do). The ones he liked, he hummed; the ones he didn't like, he discarded. One by one the parts of the composition would attach themselves to the original tune—variations, instrumentation, counterpoint—provided that nothing distracted him. "Then," wrote Mozart, "my mind seizes it as a glance of my eye seizes a beautiful picture or a handsome youth. It does not come to me successively, with its various parts worked out in detail, as they will be later on, but it is in its entirety that my imagination lets me hear it."[1] Mozart's last statement is the most interesting aspect of the letter, and what a different picture this gives of him than does the play and film *Amadeus*. His imagination lets him hear the composition. He speaks of it almost as though it were a separate entity from himself, as if imagination is distinct from his conscious self. He implies a certain graciousness on the part of his imagination, as though it censored his mental work. If it were good, Mozart would be allowed to hear it, if not, his imagination killed it. If his imagination worked that way, it might explain why he wrote so little that was not great.

Metaphors at Every Bend

Imagination not only makes images, but metaphors and symbols as well. All three are similar, yet subtly different. Each one has a slightly different structure, though each is a function of imagination. Every architect builds houses, yet each one has a unique approach to "houseness." The same is true for metaphor, symbol, and image.

A metaphor is a word picture, and unlike an image, is essentially verbal. Someone's image may need to be described to another person with words, but having an image or discovering an image happens almost instantaneously. Most people don't need to put an image into words to explain it to themselves. The image may simply exist in the mind's eye or ear. Or it lies in front of you—a cross, a fish, a sports trophy. Bringing an image to life may take effort, but not necessarily *verbal* effort. The result of a metaphor may be imagistic—that is, it may bring to mind a picture of something, an atmosphere, a sound, or texture, but it does so through words, not through objects.

All of us use metaphors. Metaphors help us see connections where there don't seem to be any. Jesus shows us how to make metaphors; we should follow his example. Although Aristotle thought that metaphoric ability was the mark of true genius, each of us, genius or not, has the ability to make metaphors. We are born with it. Accompanied by howls of delight from parents and other adults, every child exhibits this metaphoric ability, although a four-year-old has no idea that he has just invented a wonderfully funny metaphor. Unfortunately, by the time he is old enough to know what a metaphor is, his schooling may have drummed metaphoric thinking out of him. It is relegated to what poets and novelists do—which we need to study to decipher—rather than as the natural consequence of a lively imagination. In *Frames of Mind: The Theory of Multiple Intelligences*, Howard Gardner claims that an ability for metaphors is universal, found in representatives of every discipline. A four-year-old may make an analogy between ginger ale and his foot being asleep. An adult who thinks in metaphors and analogies—I am the vine, I am a road, I am water, the kingdom is like leaven, the kingdom is like a net, I am the fatted calf, I am death and life, and so forth—"will discern connections virtually everywhere and can censor those that appear unproductive or uncommunicative."[2]

In fact, just as with images, we couldn't communicate without metaphors. Language works through metaphors—our language and any other language you name. Some people may call them figures of speech, idiomatic expressions, clichés, or dead metaphors. Whatever the term, they function the same. Referring to the appendages on a chair or table as "legs" is a simple metaphor. The old saying, "applying the rod of instruction to the seat of learning," combines two metaphors—now clichés—and everyone understands what the speaker means (some of us quite intimately). "My soul thirsts for the living God" has two metaphors in it, one explicit and the other implicit. The need of the soul is expressed through a physical need—thirst—though the soul has no mouth, throat, or digestive system to swallow the drink it is thirsting for. What the parched soul wants is the living God—the implication being, as Christ points out to the woman at the well, that God is eternal and is living water. That metaphor, from the Psalms, is common throughout Scripture. The Bible uses metaphors to explain in simple, homely ways difficult spiritual concepts. Even so, theologians and preachers disagree about what they mean. What would have happened to us if God had chosen to reveal himself the way most theologians choose to reveal their ideas—in non-metaphorical language? What little insight we have as to the nature of God and man and their relationship to each other would have been missed entirely.

God is described as father, king, ruler, judge, hen, fortress, counselor, wall, rock, a still small voice, a mighty wind, a thief in the night. The list could go on and on. Many of Jesus' parables are nothing more than extended metaphors. The prodigal son is perhaps the most beautiful and well-known of these extended metaphors. Many of them describe and characterize not only the nature of human beings but also our relationship with God. "I am the vine; you are the branches" is such a metaphor. To understand it we need to ask ourselves what the statement means literally and then transfer that meaning to the spiritual realm. Christ is comparing himself to a vine and us to the branches of that vine. Those of us who think we need ministers or theologians to explain Scripture simply have not been taught to ask the right questions or to understand the nature of the rhetoric being used in a particular passage. We don't really need anyone to tell us of the relationship of trunk, branch, root, and so forth (unless, of course, we are hopelessly urban). The meaning of the metaphor in most cases reveals itself through the metaphor (another way of saying the medium is the message?). Whether or not we understand every subtlety of Jesus' metaphors is unimportant so long as we see the main point. In the case of the vine and branches, dependence and interdependence seem to be what Jesus is getting at. He is explaining a great deal about our relationship to him. That metaphor is not nearly so startling to us as his metaphor of the importunate woman and the judge. The meaning seems to be that the squeaky wheel gets the grease. Is Jesus saying that we should hound God for justice as the indefatigable woman nagged the judge night and day?

Just as we saw with images, so here with metaphors: You cannot escape them. At every bend in the language they confront us. We need not be satisfied with dead metaphors any more than we should be content with sour water. We can't extract dead metaphors from our language; nor should we want to. But we can enliven our minds and our conversations by creating new metaphors for relationships, situations, or problems. What we enjoy about certain lyricists, poets, or writers is their ability to use metaphors (even if most of us don't know that those verbal pictures are called metaphors). Metaphors startle us into new awarenesses; they help us see relationships that may have always existed but of which we were unaware. Or in explaining metaphors—such as the potter and the clay or the physical and spiritual bodies—writers help us appreciate metaphors more deeply.

Becoming Metaphor-Makers

Anyone can make up metaphors. It isn't only the province of poets. We hear them everyday; we read them in nearly every sentence. Poet and sometime sports writer Donald Hall, however, thinks we're in a "metaphor-hating society." He praises sports writer Tom Boswell of the *Washington Post* for his dexterous use of metaphor: "lizard tongue of a mitt," for example. Hall writes, "I am grateful to Tom Boswell and to the sports pages for watering the garden of metaphor in a dry time. The sports section is the only place in the paper where we are likely to find an image more complex than an adjective accompanied by a noun or a metaphor neither inadvertent nor trite nor mixed."[3] If he is right, the only metaphors we know are the dead ones, which makes it difficult for people who don't recognize a metaphor when it shakes their hand to make up some metaphors for themselves. But it also points out how much we need metaphor-makers—and not just in newspapers.

The only reason not to make your own metaphors may be timidity or self-consciousness. In the world of imagination neither has a place. But why would the average person—you or I—be creating metaphors? It isn't exactly the sort of thing a person would decide to do for the day, like getting up on Saturday to do the laundry or mow the lawn. Nevertheless, there's no reason why someone couldn't spend an hour or two putting some metaphors on paper. After all, whether we consciously write metaphors or not, each of us is, by the way we live, creating a lifelong metaphor. Perhaps that is what James meant when he said that they'll know you are Christians by the love you show one another. Scripture demands that our lives become a metaphor for justice, peace, hope, patience. It's difficult for us to act just or patient or hopeful. We approach these virtues as we would a suit of clothes that doesn't quite fit us but with a little weight loss or gain will form our frame perfectly. No wonder so many of us fail and feel guilty about our failure to walk the narrow way Christ taught. We're so concerned our clothes don't fit that we keep missing the road signs telling us which way to turn or what to do next.

However, if we think of ourselves as living metaphors of patience, hope, kindness, social justice—if, in short, we become these things—then we will not miss those yield-right-of-way or merge signs that God sends us. Becoming a metaphor is the mark of maturity for every Christian; some of us reach it sooner than others. To help us, we need to get into the habit of thinking metaphorically. Writing metaphors about various aspects of our lives is a good way to begin. (Some of the most immediate passages of the New Testament would be unintelligible without the metaphors Paul uses, as in the passage about the race and the prize or the first verse of 1 Corinthians 13. Or what about Jesus' living metaphors: I am the Way, I am the Door, I am the Living Water. We need to emulate him and be able to say I am justice, I am love, I am kindness.)

Without doubt, writing a metaphor clarifies your understanding of what you are writing the metaphor about. A person writing metaphors for his job might discover why it is he dreads going to work, for example, or what there is about it that he loves. Husbands and wives could make up metaphors about their relationship or the nature of their family life; the results could be both revealing and healing. Someone seeking to understand himself could attempt metaphors about himself. Metaphors help define a person's expectations, ambitions, hopes, dreams. They could lead to memories and images that help explain someone's current attitudes or behavior. A habit of thinking metaphorically could transform someone's working and nonworking hours from boredom and drudgery to enthusiastic vitality. Long content with mediocrity, a person might suddenly find himself searching for richer and more rewarding ways to spend his life.

In practicing this habit of metaphor, you or I may also discover why we have not become what God intended us to be. It could pinpoint persistent attitudes, unhealthy patterns, un-Christlike notions. Metaphorical thinking could even help us discover the metaphors that are controlling our lives. We might uncover the most devastating metaphor of all: I am God. The first step to health is diagnosing the disease; only then can you determine the dose of the medicine needed for a cure, not just a remission.

Most people do not live in either total darkness or total light. What we will probably find as we develop our habit of metaphorical thinking is that we live mixed metaphors like a canoe paddled up the road of life. It doesn't work; we can't mix our metaphors and expect our lives to make sense or show to parched throats where the living water is to be found. We'll end up giving meat to the thirsty, water to the starving, and stones to those who hunger for bread.

Symbols, "Statements" of Significance

If image is frequently visual and often relates to memory or some event (as in the Lord's Supper) and comes with layers of meaning and a roomful of associations, and if metaphor is a verbal linking of two at times incongruous concepts (as in Christ and a road or a lizard tongue and a mitt), then symbol combines both. A metaphor can become a symbol for a whole body of thought, a summation of a religious or theological perspective. An image, too, can be a symbol—a sign or a "statement" of significance. A crucifix, for example, could symbolize to one person an incorrect view of the gospel story while to another it might symbolize the suffering, wounded healer, and therefore be an object of mystical meditation or a reminder to live in grace. A symbol may have meaning on its own; the object that we call symbol attains a life apart from that which originally gave it significance. A symbol can remain potent (or at least recognizable) in a society or culture long after people have ceased to associate it with its origin. For example, the American eagle may no longer be associated with a warlike nation, strength, character, assertiveness, isolation, protectiveness; yet we would still recognize it as a symbol for our country (even though many Americans would not accept its view of this nation).

Although symbols can be living things, fresh and powerful in their significance, they are often no more than linguistic or visual fossils. The object remains, though the meaning has long since disappeared. Symbols can be personal or corporate; but can they really be symbols unless someone believes in them? Can a symbol be stripped of meaning and be anything but a historical relic? Belief is what transforms a mere religious symbol—the cross, for example—into an image imbued with deep theological, metaphysical, and mystical significance. Symbols can come and go with time, an image remains; it strikes closer to the heart of truth. For example, people call this the computer age. The computer is our current symbol while it once was the horse and buggy. The abacus once symbolized calculation for a society, now we have the hand held calculator. For some people, the empty tomb may just be an outmoded symbol of a once common religious belief. For other people, the empty tomb is still an image of God's love for his creatures.

The meaning of a symbol then, may not relate directly to its source, in this case, the Resurrection. The empty tomb is a symbol of the Resurrection; it is also an image of what the Resurrection means. Symbols are directly tied to an event or a person; an image to its meaning. Standing between the two are metaphors—linguistic bridges between image and symbol. You can explain symbol and image through metaphor. All three together combine in Scripture and Christianity in an attempt to explain the infinite to the finite, or as Milton put it in *Paradise Lost*, to justify the ways of God to men.

Becoming Truly Sighted

What is the point of all of this? Does it matter that we understand the differences and relationship between image, metaphor, and symbol? Yes! We cannot understand imagination until we know what imagination does. Imagination makes images, symbols, and metaphors. It makes abstract concepts meaningful and clarifies the shadowy. We can't begin to use imagination until we know its results. We cannot become living metaphors unless we know how to recognize a metaphor when it comes our way. Imagination surrounds us. It isn't enough to tell someone of the joy and glory of trees, unless we first describe a few to him. Otherwise he'll walk through a forest searching for maples, ash, birch, or oak without ever realizing they are all around him. We are like people born blind, who, when they are given sight, cannot tell an apple from an orange. They cannot see even though they have been given their sight. It takes a long adjustment for a sightless person to become truly sighted, to be able to look at objects and see more than distorted shapes and colors.

When it comes to seeing with imagination, many of us remain sightless. Others may have been given back their eyes, but their vision is still afflicted; they have yet to make the transition. Others of us are beginning to see what everyone else has been exclaiming over all along.

Image, metaphor, and symbol. The first two are the most important. We cannot be expected to create metaphors, either of ourselves or about ourselves, unless we understand what metaphors are. We use metaphors everyday; we would have to avoid reading, speaking, and listening to avoid metaphors. It's the same with images and symbols. People will invent images and symbols if they don't have any. For some reason, we need them; without images, we have no truth. If we can only recognize how embedded into our language are metaphors and how intrinsic to Christianity and the nature of God they are, then we will be able to see a little more clearly what it means to be made in the image of God and what responsibility that places on each one of us. We are image-bearers, truth-givers at birth. We are God's meaning; we are his imagination incarnated, just as Christ was his word incarnated.

All of this says a great deal about how we are to live, what we are to be. We cannot allow ourselves to walk through the forest without seeing the trees. Our mind's eye, our imagination, must be open and active. Look around. See the images of God and man. Read the metaphors. Handle the symbols. Talk to God; talk to each other; talk to nature. We can spend our lives trying to ignore his image and thus disfigure ourselves, or we can learn to recognize the metaphors and live through them. That's what theology is all about.

Chapter 3, Notes

1. Jacques Hadamard, *The Psychology of Invention in the Mathematical Field* (Princeton, 1949), p. 16.

2. Howard Gardner, *In Frames of Mind: The Theory of Multiple Intelligence* (Basic books, 1983), pp. 283-293.

3. Donald Hall, *Fathers Playing Catch with Sons* (North Point Press, 1985), p. 130.

Chapter 4

Caught in the Crack

The Knight knew he was trapped. One minute he had been talking with the Witch, the next—flattened. He felt as thin as a fingernail, well almost. He couldn't see much, either, just a deep gray-black with a hint of something that may have been yellow or gold on the horizon. A sun, perhaps, though it didn't seem to give any light, certainly no heat—just a color in the midst of this colorless world.

He sighed to himself, knowing he hadn't been the best ruler the land had ever seen, but right now he was the only ruler they had. With no son and no first-rate advisor, he knew his country would be at the Witch's mercy, and she probably didn't have any. Well, it was his fault. He'd been fooled by her pretty face—always had been a weakness. How he loved to turn a felicitous phrase.

The Knight brought himself up short. Here he was trapped, his country probably in turmoil and anguish wondering what had happened to him, and he was thinking about how melodious his voice sounded. "No wonder," he thought with disgust, "the Witch captured me so easily." The problem now was to get out of this predicament. Had he really heard her say something like, "See you in seven years, sonny?" There wouldn't be a decent dogwood or kolkwitzia left by the time he got back to Dendra, he was certain of it.

Wandering again. He couldn't seem to keep his mind on the problem. But, really, what was he supposed to do about it? He didn't know any magic. He was only half listening when the Witch put the spell on him, so he couldn't even try reversing the words to see if that would release him. He tried to move. Couldn't do it, though he did feel a little strange right down the middle, sort of breezy, as if he were divided in half. He couldn't see his hands, either. He could lower his eyes slightly, but that was all. Nothing seemed unusual—except that he was flat and trapped and in a black something or other. "Wandering," he thought again, "my mind is wandering." Yes, there it was, a slight tear, or maybe a crack.

Just as the Knight came to that conclusion, he was standing before a small boy with owlish eyes, made even rounder by oversized glasses. Next to him sat a much older girl. The child seemed somewhat surprised, the girl looked as though knights with cracked helmets were as common as weeds.

"There he is," the girl said to the little boy. "You asked for him; you got him. Now what do you want to do with him? Not that he's much good at anything in particular. I doubt that he could help you learn to read or do anything useful."

But the little boy wasn't interested in useful. He was interested in unusual. And unusual had come to him. He loved to build castles with his blocks, but he'd always lacked the main attraction—the knight.

"What's your name?" the little boy finally asked after looking him over.

If his strange travels hadn't made him cautious, that question did. "We don't give out our names, sir," he said to the child.

"Oh. Well, I'll just call you the Knight. Where'd you come from?"

"You mean, you don't know?" replied the Knight in dismay. "Then how will I get back? I was hoping you'd be able to return me to Dendra. I wasn't really too fond of being flat; round is a whole lot better. The problem is I've got this country and the Witch keeps twisting it and . . ."

"And you," interrupted the girl, "let yourself be tricked. You've got a spell on you. It sticks out a mile." Abruptly, she turned to the child at her side. "You've got to decide what we should do with him. Mother could come back any minute from grocery shopping. I don't think she'd like to find him here, not with that lance. She's not big on weapons, you know."

The Knight was thinking as rapidly as he knew how. A lot had happened in just a few minutes. First, he was in Dendra making a fool out of himself. Then he was in that strange place, kind of the same color as that ring in the girl's hand. Now he was in what seemed to be a dwelling, and these strangers were discussing what to do with him. Maybe he should try the royal approach. He *had* to get back home.

"Now wait a minute," the Knight began in his roundest tones, addressing the girl. "Apparently you brought me here just to amuse this odd-looking child. Pretty rude, if you ask me. No castle governess would ever consider such a thing. Boredom is the hallmark of civilized behavior. Besides, I am the ruler, Knight of Dendra. My land is in jeopardy from a despicable witch, and I must return as quickly as possible. Now. I command you to send me back."

This was quite a rousing speech. The Knight ended it with a great flourish of his lance and a clank of his armor. Of course, he knocked his helmet askew with his lance and stubbed his toe on the coffee table when he tried to click his heels, but all in all it was a pretty good effort at royal indignation.

He was astonished when the girl replied, "Are you sure Dendra is in that much danger? Maybe you don't know the Witch as well as you think you do."

Chapter 5

The Metaphor-Maker

If most of us find ourselves walking through life with our imaginations unchallenged, unstimulated, or virtually non-existent, it may be because we have no models of imaginative living. We are not encouraged to see imaginatively, nor do we study the lives of those men and women who have exercised and developed their imaginations. Certainly our educational system, with its desire to be pragmatic or original, does its best to rid us of any shred of imaginative impulse. Remember, I am not talking about "creativity," that much ballyhooed word in public education. English teachers have forsaken grammar, spelling, punctuation, and literature to encourage students from junior high on to "be creative," to write what they feel. Yet the average thirteen-year-old is too young to be able to do those things—there aren't many Miltons around today.

In an effort to convince American educators that imagination is something each of us has, and that we should not destroy it in the process of educating our children, Mary Warnock published a book with the University of California Press called *Imagination*. In it she defines imagination as "a power in the human mind which is at work in our everyday perception of the world, and is also at work in our thoughts about what is absent;

which enables us to see the world, whether present or absent, as significant, and also to present this vision to others, for them to share or reject."[1]

The Gospel and Once-Upon-a-Time

Warnock's words have obvious implications for our theology. We cannot have faith (belief in that which is unseen) unless we have imagination; imagination is the vehicle through which faith is expressed. Nor can we understand our world without active imaginations—our world view that sees God as creator and controller, caretaker and lover. How can we present our vision of the world and how life should be lived if we cannot move from our imagination to that of an unbelieving imagination? People want stories; we give them systems, dull postulations. Galileans responded to Jesus because he entertained them as he taught them. The only way to apprehend a mystery is through imagination. Our metaphors and paradoxes attempt to make concrete—at least a little—the faith presented in Scripture. With apologies to the systematic theologians, systems of theology leave people with thirsts unsatisfied. A treatise on the virgin birth can never have the power of the image of the baby Jesus, God incarnate, in a hay trough. Our theologians should tell us stories; I'm certain they should read more stories to find out how it's done. I would like to hear . . .

> Once upon a time, God wanted to send his people a present. So he shopped everywhere for just the right gift. But though he looked in all the places he could think of, he couldn't find anything that suited the stubborn, quixotic, and yet charming part of his creation he called mankind. These creatures meant a lot to him; how could he show he cared?
>
> Then one day he looked casually to his right and saw his son, a pretty sharp guy. Now if there was anything or anyone he loved more than his wayward creation, it was his steadfast son. We've all experienced times when what we've been looking for has

been right in front of us all along. Well, God suddenly had that feeling. What better gift to show you care than by giving what you care about most? In his imagination, God saw his son and his creatures meeting each other for the first time. Jesus was sure getting the royal treatment—the best calf butchered for him, the gold plate, the silver flatware, the crystal goblets. Hmmm, God muttered to himself. He imagined the faces of the people staring at Jesus—eyes glazed over, lips tightly smiling, stress lines about the mouth. No real relationships there. Everyone was just trying to impress Jesus, not getting to know him or his father through him.

God knew right then that it would never do to send Jesus as he was. He needed to disguise him as a poor, younger brother, the kind the fairy tales talk about. True, thought God to himself as he watched his son talk to some visitors, there are risks that way, too. Some people won't talk to him because his community standing won't be very high. But those who do—well, they'll discover what a great guy he is without being dazzled by his pedigree. What I'm after, he thought, is relationship. So . . .

God sent his son wrapped in swaddling clothes and laid him in a manger because there was no room for him at the inn.

What does once-upon-a-time do for us? What does a story say that systematics cannot? Why did I end with familiar words from Luke rather than the genealogy of Matthew? Luke was telling Theophilus a story; that is the reason why Luke's gospel is read at Christmas. I'm not claiming that my short example is the best story ever, but I think it shows some possibilities. People would rather read things written as stories, even things that are true. We want that once-upon-a-time framework; it says that at this time, some past time, or no time at all, the following occurred. It puts the story in the universal mode immediately, yet it is a particular story about specific people and what they said and did. Once upon a time also means that the story could be taking place in our time as well as any other. Since no one knows when time began, "In the beginning God created" has that same once-upon-a-time feel.

The point of my story is true, though the details may be questionable. God sent us a gift, his Son, the most imaginative person who ever lived. No storyteller, no matter how gifted, could have come up with a more dramatic approach. A young, innocent girl is shocked and interrupted in her daily chores by a heavenly messenger, probably a pretty frightful or awesome character in his own right. I'm going to have a baby? she thinks. If she's like most young girls, even today, she probably knew very little about sex and reproduction. But she accepts the burden—all pregnancies are in one way or another a burden—and she and Joseph set up house. How could a storyteller top that first chapter? Yet the story only gets better. Politics enters; as is the way of government, it interferes with the plans of ordinary people, which always hinge on being left alone. So off goes Mary, nearly nine months pregnant and sick of being that way. She and Joseph reach their destination after an arduous trip only to have Mary immediately go into labor. (Who knows— the trip could have brought on the labor.) No doctor, no hospital, probably no hot water or clean cloths. Having a baby in a taxi is nothing compared to Mary's experience. What a way to start life; and yet, for a person of imagination, no way more fitting.

Not only do the plot and setting of the story reflect imagination, but also the characters. Joseph, too, had to exercise his imagination to believe what he was told. He had to exercise a willing suspension of disbelief that Mary's child did not come about in the ordinary way. Much of what God asks us to believe requires imagination—we need to perceive that what we see may not be the whole story. Remember what Jesus told Thomas: blessed are those who have not seen and yet believe. Unfortunately, some people just become too sophisticated to exercise their imaginations. C. S. Lewis makes the same point in the Narnia Chronicles. Susan doesn't get into the real Narnia at death because as an adult she dismissed her belief in Narnia as mere childhood imaginings and therefore untrue. Jesus asks us never to do that. On the contrary, he insists that each of us become a child again in order to enter the kingdom of heaven. He made a point of saying this in a day when children were even lowlier than women. No one took children seriously, though male children were important for the future. Childhood was a frivolous time. But Jesus saw that children have a remarkable strength and resilience of imagination (a characteristic that is becoming more and more difficult to find in children). To children all things are possible—lands like Narnia, creatures like Aslan or Santa Claus. Children also know, somehow without being told, which of their beliefs are made-up and which are true, which ones to discard—Santa Claus, for example—and which ones to retain—Jesus watching over me.

Unfortunately, Jesus' biographers skip most of his childhood, with the exception of his family's trip to Jerusalem when he was twelve. Of his adult life, though, we have ample evidence of his great imaginative ability. Jesus was imagination incarnate because he was God incarnate. His life tells us a lot about what it means to have our lives informed by imagination. We can see Jesus' imagination at work in three primary areas: in his miracles, in his parables, and in his relationships.

These three areas are inextricably woven together. Jesus often performed miracles because he responded to the people around him. Either he imaginatively empathized with their suffering or he recognized their strong imaginative vision that he could accomplish what he chose. He was also teaching his followers a lesson. The same is true for his parables; he chose the most appropriate imaginative form to help kindle the people's imagination. Jesus' oft-repeated phrase, "He who has ears to hear, let him hear," is not only an appeal for understanding, but is also an appeal to the mind's ear.

Miracles and Metaphors

Jesus was a metaphor-maker; he thought and taught in images, symbols, and stories. He wasn't a great novelist or poet, yet the same imagination that marks the lives of artists was present in Jesus. He practiced imaginative living and was constantly calling his listeners to do the same. His miracles, too, seem to be a product of imagination. Not the ability to do them; that came from God; but the ability to understand what miracle was needed and why the person was asking for it. Look at his first miracle, turning water into wine at the feast of Cana.

John gives us an interesting picture of Jesus' relationship with his mother. She had been invited to a wedding, as had Jesus and his friends. Undoubtedly, they were having a good time in an all-male way when Jesus' mother interrupts them to complain that the host has run out of wine, which was a serious breach of the laws of hospitality. Easterners don't like to lose face. Mary obviously assumes that if he chooses, Jesus can do something about the wine situation. He, on the other hand, is just as obviously not interested. He gives his mother an excuse—"my time has not yet come"—but she ignores the remark, telling the servants to do whatever Jesus tells them. Mothers know an excuse when they hear one. And sons know that they know, so Jesus turned some jugs of water into wine. He recognized why his mother had come to him; they understood each other.

Jesus also understood the significance of metaphors, symbols, and images, those things that imagination creates. Food and drink carried great imaginative weight in the Middle East (as well as being universal images of health, well-being, and contentment). Many of Jesus' stories, metaphors, and miracles deal with banqueting, weddings, feasting, celebration. At the Last Supper he made himself the incarnate image of bread and wine, the staples of life. Jesus becomes the staples, so that physically and spiritually we cannot live without him. He's the only market in town. The miracle at Cana beautifully foreshadows Passover. Jesus recognized the imaginative value of turning water into wine for his first miracle. Through his death water led to blood, which in turn became our wine, a heady drink, the holiest of mysteries.

Water, wine, and blood all flow together, becoming one. "Is there a difference?" Jesus seems to be asking. Each in its own way shares strength-giving, life-sustaining properties; through imagination they partake of the same meaning from the same source, the love of the Creator and the celebration of the Son. Jesus begins and ends his ministry with the same images, the food of life and celebration. The ordinary and the celebratory spring from the same source: one is water, the other wine. Straddling the two is Christ's blood, which makes both the ordinary and the celebratory meaningful. Christ's blood mysteriously makes the ordinary a celebration and the celebratory an everyday event; life becomes whole. His blood removes the partitions. Jesus knew where he was heading when he turned the water into wine. He knew celebration was only part of the story, that suffering fit in, too. Yet celebration was no insignificant part; so despite his irritation at being interrupted, he did what he recognized imaginatively his mother was asking: He provided the wine as one day he would provide the blood.

The crucifixion was also an interruption. Jesus didn't want death; he was human enough to deny it. The idea of death nearly proved too much even for his imagination. Yet because he had a disciplined imagination, he was able in the Garden of Gethsemane to pray for his father's will to be accomplished. The miracle of the Resurrection was accomplished first in the imagination of God. Mythologies of all cultures contain stories of gods dying and rising again. God placed in man's imagination the desire to conquer death and the willingness to believe in its possibility. People everywhere have the same imaginative vision of the gods defeating death. What marks the Christian reality from mythology (apart from the fact that it actually happened) is the reason for our God dying and rising again.

Not every miracle is imbued with as much imagery as the miracle at Cana. They do, however, fall into discernible patterns that relate to Christ's own experiences: from the water into wine at Cana to the sweat-like blood at Gethsemane to the wine that is his blood at the Last Supper to the blood and water flowing together on the cross, with neither water nor wine given the thirsty, dying man but rather vinegar, like wine that has been kept too long. The day of wine had ended for him. Jesus' feeding the five thousand foreshadows the Last Supper as surely as does the feast at Cana. Jesus multiplied the meager food to fill the hungry to contentment. Jesus broke bread at the Last Supper to fill his disciples with himself. At the crucifixion he fed more people than a mere five thousand with the bread of life.

Most people don't think of Jesus' miracles as images or metaphors. But just as Jesus was God incarnate, which includes the imagination of God, so his deeds were incarnated. He was the Word. He was the Image, the Symbol, the Metaphor, the Meaning. Each of his miracles, then, was more than wonder-working. It was an image, a symbolic representation of some aspect of his life and ministry. Cana and feeding the five thousand are images of the Last Supper and crucifixion. His miracles of raising the dead obviously foreshadow his own triumph over death for all of us. As man-God he could reach people individually—healing a few, raising some from the dead, feeding others—yet as God-man in his glorified state he reached us all.

Jesus healed the blind, the deaf, the leprous; he brought the outcasts of society into the mainstream of Palestinian life. He cured the acutely ill as well as the chronically ill. Yet he cast out—verbally, at least (though his words symbolize a future act)—those who lived at the very heart of Jewish religious life, the Pharisees, Sadducees, lawyers, rabbis, and priests. He knew they were not just people, but whitewashed sepulchers, a marvelously imaginative image. For Jesus, people had lasting, imaginative meaning. They were either good seed or bad, either fruitful fig trees or barren, either wise architects or foolish. He helped people understand themselves through images, metaphors, and symbols. He constantly asked people, Which image are you? Which metaphor will characterize your life? Are you the persistent widow? The good Samaritan? The mustard seed? The prodigal son? The field hand? Some of his implicit questions came in the form of parables, stories; others were

merely short sentences, almost idle asides as he and his followers walked the shores of Galilee. You cannot turn a page in the
Gospels without reading marvelous images, powerful metaphors,
stirring symbols. Jesus leaves none of us out; there is an image
there for every one of us—sometimes several. He knew one
image would not suffice because every imagination works differently and therefore is captured by different images. For some
people, urban images work better than country images or feasting better than fasting.

An Imagination Fully Awake

Yet, most people never know whether to take images literally or figuratively. Images and metaphors confuse people, even
though they are, as Jesus knew, the best way to understand anything. In this he troubled, confused, and frightened people.
They didn't know what to make of his healing the centurion's
daughter or raising Lazarus from the dead. Certainly they were
unprepared for the Resurrection. The Pharisees didn't realize
Jesus was referring to his body when he threatened to tear down
the temple and rebuild it in three days. They were using the
organ of reason, not the organ of truth. The physical building
was not the real temple—that was only a physical representation
of what lives in God's imagination. Jesus' body was the meaning for which the temple stood, and therefore more real than the
temple building itself. Thus he could say that his body would be
torn down and that God would rebuild it in three days. Although
reason and imagination are not enemies or opponents, they
sometimes do conflict. Reason may give us one interpretation,
imagination another; God informs both and desires that they
work together. But the Gospels show many people who misun-
derstood Jesus simply because they were seeing him with closed
imaginations.

This is certainly the case not only with the religious and
political leaders of the day, but also with Jesus' closest followers. The disciples consistently misinterpreted Jesus' behavior.
They tried to remove the children as a nuisance when they
flocked around Jesus. They resented the help he gave to the

centurion. They tried to protect him from the clamoring masses of people who followed him once they had heard about his miracles. Some of what he taught they did understand. The disciples' imagination worked after a fashion. Peter could confess Jesus was the Messiah. Still, the disciples expected an earthly messiah, a completely Jewish messiah—not a spiritual ruler who came for everyone. It was almost as if they wanted Jesus to belong to them, resenting intrusions into their group.

One difference between Jesus and his followers—or Jesus and any of the rest of us—is that he was fully awake. His imagination was active regardless of how tired he was or how many people demanded answers. The woman with the hemorrhage merely had to touch the hem of his robe. He knew what had happened; so did she. Jesus tried to teach his disciples how to remain awake while the rest of society slept—perhaps occasionally stirred by uneasy dreams, but never waking up enough to look for the answer. The Garden of Gethsemane provides a striking example. Jesus asked his disciples to watch and pray. He himself was tormented by his future. The disciples, however, not imagining his anguish, fell asleep. Other would-be followers had been easily discouraged by Jesus' realistic picture of his life and that of his followers. "Foxes and birds have homes, but not I," said Jesus. "Picture that kind of life before you make promises you can't keep," he said. Imagine it. Put yourself mentally in that place. Jesus knew the unseen order of life; he had created it. He saw life whole. His reason for existence infused everything he did or said. He didn't compartmentalize life into work, play, relationships, secular life, spiritual life. He knew that all life was sacred and that every person had the possibility to live in harmony with Creator and creation through grace-filled imagination. (Because we lack that ability, we must dissect life to understand it; but we need to try to put the pieces back together once we have dissected it. For most of us, it's like trying to put Humpty Dumpty back together.)

That is why Jesus' life shows the patterns it does. There are no isolated incidents. Although Jesus was God Incarnate, he is our model: we can become like him. We may not be able to perform nature-breaking miracles, but we can see the miraculous happen in everyday fashion. Every person we encourage, every unselfish act, every metaphor we make up, and every image we live through can miraculously change lives—ours and those around us. Our imagination can grow through stimulation and use, just as the physical brain can. Through experiments with rats, scientists have discovered that an animal with little early stimulation has a stunted brain. Yet this stunting can be reversed. The brain can grow with exercise, just as the muscles of the body will expand with regular physical exertion. Because a rat's brain has two sides, scientists assume that the same thing happens to us. Psychologists and teachers can confirm this. Children raised in non-intellectually stimulating environments and who show little interest in books and learning can change if given a different environment. Just as children need love to mature, they also need food for their imaginations; unfortunately, too many children are not getting the food they need.

Parables and Patterns

Through his parables, Jesus was trying to expand the imaginations of his followers. Jesus' miracles sprang from his compassion or occasionally to satisfy the people's longings for a sign. He knew that in the days ahead they would need all the strength possible—physical, emotional, and spiritual. An understanding imagination—one that was able to complete the story—would comfort them as they watched Jesus suffer and die.

I've already mentioned some of the better known examples of the metaphors Jesus used for himself—vine, way, light. Many of his parables are merely extended metaphors, though some of them, the prodigal son, for example, are also stories. As we study the New Testament, it's difficult to find a place where Jesus did not speak in metaphors, similes, and parables. He used the stuff of everyday life; the characters in his stories are those his audience would have known, in some cases would probably have had deep emotional responses to:

landlords, land owners, absentee farmers, vintners, wealthy
men who built ever larger outbuildings, overseers who exacted
plenty of work for little pay. Jesus knew his audience—the
poor, the sick, the maimed, the outcast of Palestinian society—
and he knew they wanted to hear about wealthy, unjust people
who got their comeuppance. An oppressed group of black
people today would relish a story about The Man whom the
Lord sent to hell because he refused to give the crumbs from his
table to the starving. Jesus would never have gone along with
the "art for art's sake" school; he understood that art imitates
life and thereby teaches people moral lessons. More so than any
other aspect of his life, Jesus' words give clear evidence that he
understood the importance of imagination.

At the same time that Jesus told stories of the wealthy, he
also admonished his audience to be merciful and to show justice. He squelched the pride in every listener with stories of trees
bearing good and bad fruit or men who build foolishly or wisely.
He showed that not only business men can be unjust, but so can
underlings, as in the man whose large debt was forgiven by his
boss but who turned around and demanded a small sum from a
poor man who owed him some money. What listener couldn't
identify with the story of the speck of sawdust and the plank. At
one time, every one of us has looked critically at neighbor,
friend, or relative when our eyesight has been cloudy; at best we
suffer from scratched corneas and detached retinas.

Jesus' parables still have the same zing and barb they had
when he first spoke them, and that despite the drastic changes in
knowledge, perception, culture, and lifestyle. Not many of us
work in a vineyard or grow fig trees for a living. We certainly
haven't seen any Roman soldiers garrisoned anywhere near our
homes. Yet the universality of his metaphors is unmistakably
and uncomfortably close to home. Chaucer, Milton, Donne,
Herbert, Hardy, or even Eliot may need to be translated for us,
but not Jesus. Quasars, computers, and wave particles have no
more or less meaning to us than does the tale of the Good
Samaritan. People don't really need to know who the Samari-
tans were and what their relationship to the Jews was to under-

stand the story. The context makes it clear that for whatever reason he was an unlikely character to help an injured Jew. Nor do we need to know anything about the priests and the Levites to know that they should have willingly helped an injured man. It may be interesting to know the background, but Jesus has said all that is necessary. We know we would hesitate to care for someone as the Samaritan did. Although we might stop to help someone who is hurt, would we pay his medical bills? No, we are more likely to look for his major medical card to find out if his group insurance policy will cover the treatment he needs. We certainly don't want to be stuck with the expenses. We have enough bills of our own. But that's taking the story too literally, right?

Justice, mercy, compassion, forgiveness. These are all abstract, moral, ethical concepts that philosophers write about in the most dispassionate, abstruse, and unimaginative prose possible. Reading or hearing about morality in a context divorced from people is not only dull but a waste of time. Jesus knew that. That's why he talked about people, why he gave examples, told stories, spoke in metaphors, images, and symbols. Even without the stories in the short, simple expository passages—he spoke metaphorically. Jesus didn't want anyone to escape or to excuse himself. When he was accused of doing miracles through the power of Beelzebub, Jesus didn't preach a three-point sermon or take several minutes to go into the theological understanding of who Satan is and how he operates. Rather, he said in effect, "Use your common sense; a house divided against itself will collapse." Short but to the point. Nonsense need not be dignified by taking it seriously; Jesus handled it well by telling stories that pointed out the nonsense more clearly than any debate could have. He showed wit and humor as well as perception. Those characteristics are nonexistent without imagination.

Sometimes, too, a little exaggeration helps to show imagination at work. Exaggeration, like satire (which is the formal use of exaggeration and nonsense), grabs the listener's attention. Jesus' story of the laborers hired at different times but who received the same wage is surely exaggeration. No employer would make such an agreement, though it shows what kind of an employer God is. Here if anywhere we see the irrational bounty and grace of God. It's his show, and though we may not like it, if he wants to pay the latecomers as much as those of us who showed up on time, that's his business; but it's no way to run one. Jesus also used exaggeration in the prodigal son story. The protagonist had to be very poor indeed to care for pigs and share their food, the father very forgiving. Before his son could ask, the father said, "Don't give it another thought. I've completely forgotten any differences we might have had."

The audience got the point. Promiscuity and indiscriminate living could lead to degradation, but a father's love can out exaggerate even this son's outrageous behavior. The father could forgive more than the son could commit; he was always a step ahead.

Jesus often exaggerated when necessary, particularly when the story explained the nature of God. The parable of the great banquet is another good example—a host whose friends, neighbors, and acquaintances *all* refused to come to a party? It's an unlikely scenario. Yet, as with all good storytellers, Jesus helps us suspend our disbelief by the strength of the whole parable. He appeals to our imaginations by saying, in effect, "just suppose . . ." or "just imagine that you planned a great feast but everyone you invited turned you down on some flimsy excuse or other." Even the poorest person understood then, and we still do to some extent, the role of hospitality. What terrible manners those potential guests had. But the host had party fever, and if no one else would come, he would invite anyone and everyone: strangers, beggars, poor men, ugly women, the crippled, blind, and lame. Here is God, temperature above 104 degrees, heaven-bent on having a party. In Jesus' mouth, exaggeration works.

The Word and Words

Every parable, simile, or metaphor Jesus spoke could be analyzed as I have done with these few examples. Nearly every one of Jesus' words contains some image or figure of speech.

His imagination informed everything he said or did and radiated from him to those around him. Even when his disciples were puzzled as to what he was talking about and asked him directly, "What do you mean? We don't get it," he frequently answered them with . . . another story. "If you don't get my stories, how will you understand my words without them?" Jesus asks, in effect. John calls Jesus the Word, Logos incarnate. When we think about what that means, we probably have an image of Reason, Logic, Grammar, Syllogism—something as Greek as the word Logos itself. This is the standard interpretation. However, in comparing the Word with his words—and how can you separate them?—we find something different. Jesus wasn't the master of syllogism, but of imagination, story, character, plot, simile, image, symbol. As he talked, he created worlds within this one.

Jesus' original creation is anything but colorless. He created the world to appeal to the people he intended to create. Not many of us would be content with gray lands. Not many of us are content with the color and variety of the land we have now; but things could be worse. Psychologists and cognitive scientists now know that certain people are greatly affected by grayness in weather; fog, clouds, mist, rain, all those variations we get when the sun doesn't shine. Portland, Oregon, would never do for some people. When the sun doesn't shine, nothing looks particularly colorful. Light is essential for color to appear at its best. Just as Jesus touches each of us in his parables, metaphors, and images, he touches each of us with some part of his creation. For those who like deserts, we've got deserts. For those who like oak and elm, you can find them. And everyone knows that there are dog people and cat people. Jesus told a creation story to suit every person, just as he told many kinds of parables to capture as many people as possible with his message. His words contain all the shape, texture, color, and odor that any of us could want. It's all here; he who has the eyes of imagination to see, let him see.

Christ is the only person in all of Scripture who consistently talks of himself in metaphorical terms. Others use metaphors, but not in referring to themselves. Paul uses metaphors in explaining the gospel to new Christians and old: present yourselves a living sacrifice; you are like children requiring milk and not meat; put on the whole armor of God; the church is like a body with hands, feet, head. James, too, uses a few images at the beginning of his book, for example, "he will pass away like a wildflower." But for the most part he is not strong in images. The New Testament writers may encourage us to become metaphors for God, but they seldom claim metaphors for themselves. Paul's definition of himself as a slave of the gospel is perhaps the exception to that; it has become such a cliché that it is hard to remember its original impact. The Old Testament prophets use a catalog of metaphors. God called one, Hosea, to become the living image of his message by marrying Gomer, an adulterous woman. We can be grateful that God seldom makes such requests. Becoming a positive metaphor is hard enough.

Imagination is, literally, image making. Christ is our best example of this image-making function. He made images and at the same time was image incarnate—the image of God. We, too, are to be an image of God. We're made that way, but in us the image is cracked, distorted, painted with some garish color. When Paul says that we will become like Jesus, the first fruits, this is what he means. The image of God will be restored to us. God will strip off the cheap paint to reveal the natural patina and image that was there all the time. Probably the most we can hope to do until then is to chip away the paint, a little here, a little there, and try to prevent additional coats of paint from being applied. It is unquestionably a painful process for us. Aslan in *The Voyage of the Dawn Treader* turns Eustace Scrubb, a dragon of a child, literally into a dragon. Then Eustace had to let Aslan peel away the layers of dragon skin to recover the little boy who was there all the time. It was agony for Eustace, but with the removal of each successive layer, he felt so much better. This, too, is an image of what God does with us.

God is not against images; his commandment is against idols. Jesus was an image of God. Because God is difficult to see, he was also an image of those things on earth that we all understand: a mother hen with her chicks, a healer, a lover, a shepherd, a caretaker. Although Christ said that he came to bring a sword, not peace, most of the images that he used of himself are ones of comfort, hope, tenderness, growth. He lived those images as well as talked of them. In that, too, he is our first model of how to live imaginatively. He cared for his followers with the supervision of a shepherd, the gentle touch of a good general practitioner, and the patience of a parent who also knows when to discipline his wayward children.

Relationships and Living Sacrifices

Jesus' relationships showed his imagination at work. A shepherd doesn't favor his male sheep over his female sheep. Each is important to him; he knows each by name and they know him. Jesus reflected this same respect toward women and men. Mary and Martha, Mary Magdalene, the woman at the well, the woman taken in adultery, his own mother were all treated as individuals who mattered as much as did Peter or John. He showed this same respect to other, less acceptable, people in Palestinian culture: Roman soldiers, tax collectors, publicans, sinners. For example, he knew that Zacchaeus only needed someone to show him a little human kindness and respect to become a different person. Jesus invited himself to dinner at Zacchaeus's house. Today we might say that his empathic powers were highly developed. They were. But we can't have empathy for another person unless we have an imagination willing and able to forget self and think about someone else. An empathetic person must encourage others in image making; he must help develop the rose or the elm that another person can become.

Jesus identified with everyone he met; he knew their names, knew the images they were creating. His empathetic responses were great. He knew that he could produce the same images—good or bad; he had the potential to be the woman at the well. He saw the center of a person, the place from which all the images he builds for himself begins. A tree can look sound and yet be black or hollow at its core. Other trees may look scarred or gnarled on the outside, but be green and growing, filled with good wood at the center. Jesus knew the good trees from the bad. When we think about this characteristic, and because he was God incarnate, we may imagine that he was a mindreader. Not so. He was illumined by God through his imagination, and his imagination, stretched taut and strong, helped him see what others missed because all the suppleness of their imagination was busy with themselves. Jesus' imagination was outward-functioning. He was unconcerned with developing his potential or fulfilling himself as a person. He would not fit in our society today but would be considered hopelessly old-fashioned. He used his imagination to help anticipate the needs of others and thus fulfill them—not himself. Some people needed firmness, some anger; others needed forgiveness or encouragement. He used his finely tuned imagination to fill all needs, regardless of what it cost himself. And for our ultimate need—that of grace—Jesus provided his entire being.

Jesus' relationships with people stand as a bridge between his miracles and his parables. Jesus would not have known what images to make, what metaphors to create, what stories to tell without an ability to know what his listeners needed. Living like Christ, then, means in part to live with the same imaginative intensity that he did. This is what Paul meant when he told the Romans to present their bodies a living sacrifice. Jesus wasn't a living sacrifice only on Golgotha; he was a living sacrifice every day.

While Jesus was on earth, not a day went by that someone didn't need him to be a sacrifice for them. People needed him to sacrifice sleep, comfort, security, money, strength, love, and convention. We are in that same position, though we may not recognize it. Our images may not accommodate others. We may be porcelain when pottery is needed. People may need laughter when we give tears. Jesus gave what was needed because his image was servant, shepherd. His images were always in the context of relationships, whether it was a vine to branches or a hen to her chicks or a road to a weary traveler. His miracles and his parables reflected his relationships—were images of his images, if you will. Not only do we need to become more imaginative, more image-conscious, but once we do, we then need to bring our images and imaginations into focus with the original.

Chapter 5, Notes

1. Mary Warnock, *Imagination* (University of Chicago Press, 1976), p. 196.

Chapter 6

Alice's Affliction

J esus was a *what-if* person, a *why-not* person. What if this man could walk? What if this leper were healed? What if the people didn't cry out—would the stones? Why not touch his robe? These are the questions Jesus and others asked. He had the spirit of change about him, a curiosity about people and situations. He wasn't content to hear, "But we've always done it this way." He not only changed the way, he changed "it." Whatever the "it" is in your life or mine, when Jesus enters, he transforms it. This is imagination in action.

Although Jesus is the foremost model, we need to see other people who live imaginatively. It's one thing to see God incarnate do it; it's quite another to see our neighbor or our colleague. Jesus may be the first model of imaginative living, but we can't perform miracles as he did, though we may be able to tell parables and stories or approximate the kinds of relationships he had. We need other models.

Fortunately, God has provided us with lots of them—people who have exercised the *imago Dei*. Much to our theological chagrin, however, these people have not all been Christians. That doesn't bother God—common grace is, after all, common, ordinary—but it upsets our notions of rightness.

65

We'll need to put that aside when we look at people—writers, scientists, and others—who have lived imaginative lives. There are some notable examples: Madeleine L'Engle, Chaim Potok, P. L. Travers, Astrid Lindgren, Albert Einstein, Henri Poincaré, Isaac Newton, the neighbor next door—some familiar, some not so well-known perhaps, but all with something in common, an active imagination and a similar way of working. We will discover, when we finish looking at each of these people, that a pattern has emerged.

It may seem unusual to name a scientist or a mathematician under a list of imaginative people. Writers or poets we recognize, but mathematicians? What does "it's either right or wrong" have to do with imagination? Metaphors and images seem to have nothing to do with numbers (at least for me). Our assumptions about science and scientists may not be totally accurate, however. Today when we look for imagination we may not find it in the same places we would have fifty or a hundred years ago. People with imagination are a mixed bag at best. The most unlikely characters—on the surface—have the most startling imaginations, Thomas Edison, for example. Quite ordinary people may be as imaginative as quite extraordinary people. We can—and should—learn from both. Anyone who lives an imaginative life can be an example, whether or not we can duplicate the results of his or her imagination. A Nobel Prize may not be in the offing for me or for you, but something better is: an awakened imagination, better relationships, a deeper knowledge of grace, and a clearer understanding of why we are here, as Sue Petersen discovered.

To some people, Susan knew, *ordinary* was a dirty word. People resisted being ordinary. They wanted to stand out—if only in a small crowd—from other people. People took such elaborate means to appear unusual. But, thought Susan with a little sigh and shake of her head, it was the outlandishly ordinary rather than the exquisitely extraordinary that people preferred. That was certainly true of her next door neighbor and best friend, Jeanne. Sometimes Susan wondered how they had ended up as friends, they were such opposites.

Sue preferred simple things—ordinary clothes, straightforward furniture, soft colors. Jeanne told her she had no flair. Bold orange stripes up a beige staircase wall might be all right for an inexpensive motel, but not for a house. Jeanne believed in creativity; she preached it constantly. Since Susan didn't want any part of bright orange or scarlet appliances or fuzzy wall paper, she avoided creativity with the agility of a gymnast. Their homes were quite a contrast—and not only in their color schemes.

Jeanne and her family always seemed on the edge either of a crisis or a major project: refinishing all the furniture from cherry to light oak right at Christmas or bailing out one of Jeanne's numerous relatives whose latest business venture had failed, not from want of creativity but of practicality—at least it seemed so to Susan. Or Jeanne's children were experiencing a new musical instrument or hobby that would change their lives, though at the ages of eight, ten, and thirteen creative writing and expressionist dance classes hardly seemed appropriate to Susan. That was better, though, than always sitting in front of a television or playing video games until their eyes bugged out.

People—Jeanne in particular—called Susan old-fashioned. That wasn't always the case, but several years ago she and Jack decided to severely restrict TV to an occasional baseball or football game and to monitor what records the kids borrowed from the library or listened to on the radio. They began guiding their children to good books that were not only well-written but were challenging and entertaining. For Susan, this was a big job. She had read as a child—Nancy Drew and Cherry Ames, mostly—but knew little about contemporary children's books or the classics. So she got busy and hounded library and librarians, as well as the local bookstore for reference material on children's literature. She and Jack learned a lot in the process. They instituted a reading rule, though they no longer needed to enforce it. Their children loved to read, fantasy and biography, in particular.

At first, the kids seemed just the same, though a little grumpy about no Saturday morning cartoons. But as time went on, Susan and her husband, as well as the kids' teachers, noticed a difference in the children's behavior, their vocabulary, their increased ability to concentrate. John and Laura seemed to suffer less from boredom, inventing games or telling and retelling scary stories in the dark to each other and their friends. They were also learning to figure things out on their own—how to organize their homework better or practice a difficult scale on the piano. They certainly whined and moaned less about what they didn't have—no Atari, no VHS.

Her children's friends seemed listless and out of focus without things around them. John and Laura spent hours inventing ways to entertain themselves. They showed an eagerness to learn, to discover new ideas, and to keep an open mind when confronted with a new subject. When she and Jack agreed to curtail television, it seemed like such a simple thing to do. They had also begun reading aloud together every night. Each one took turns picking books, and as the kids got to be better readers, each of them took turns reading aloud. They read the Nesbitt books, Mary Poppins, Tolkien, the Smiley Pool series, Dickens. It was natural to add to the nightly reading a chapter or two from the Bible. Everything they read stretched their imaginations in some way; they had new ideas for play or work, a new understanding of life. Jack had a new perspective on situations at work, of personnel problems or difficult colleagues. The books they read together gave him a better awareness of people's psychology and a greater empathic ability—much better than any management course he had been given by the company. Susan understood her children a little better simply by hearing the sorts of situations and dialogue to which her children had the greatest response. The Nesbitt books in particular, stories where the adults were all but absent, presented a realistic view of how children think—even though they had been written at the turn of the century.

The family benefited as a unit, as well as individually. Reading together strengthened their bond, gave them shared imaginative experiences, just as travel did or those few special traditions and celebrations they had developed over the years.

Reading also gave the family new ideas for celebrations other than the usual Christmas, Thanksgiving, and birthday parties. The family began to notice other points of view; they asked why and how and why-not questions. Their mental energy level increased dramatically.

Susan enthusiastically told her friends and neighbors about their limiting television and taking up reading. She was surprised that her neighbors thought she attributed too much to reading. Susan suggested they try it for a month or two to see what might happen. Maybe it was just her family.

Sue noticed something else. Whether it was because her children's curiosity and imagination had increased or whether her husband seemed more alert to his home surroundings, she didn't know. But days that used to stagger by now seemed filled with interest. Susan had more time to devote to Bible study, community service through her church, such hobbies as counted cross-stitch, knitting, and other handwork. She also gave more thought to meals and other normal homemaking functions. She and Jack had thought it only fair to limit television for themselves if they were going to do that with the children. So no more soap operas.

Susan began to study the piano again. The more she immersed herself in the music of Haydn, Mozart, or Chopin—if only for a half hour—the more her imagination grew. Even scales and arpeggios helped. To think about what the composer had heard when he wrote a particular sonata or mazurka, to have the rhythms and harmonies extend from the imagination through fingers and onto the keyboard, and to venture her own interpretations regardless of the editor's markings, simultaneously exhilarated and relaxed Susan. She soon discovered that practicing a half hour to an hour before the children came home from school helped prepare her to face a barrage of questions. John and Laura told exciting stories of what went on at school as a ploy to wheedle her into letting them skip piano "just this once" or wait until after supper to begin homework. As they heard her practice on weekends—she tried to get in a little time each day regardless of the family's schedule—they saw what she'd been lecturing them about since they began music lessons. John and Laura saw someone practice diligently, make mistakes without tantrums, work slowly and patiently to get a phrase just right. They began to practice with a different attitude; she watched them approach difficult school work with less fuss or tears. Here, if anywhere, she saw the truth that what parents do is more important than what they say.

Imagination, Susan decided, was similar to spices and herbs in cooking. Food could be bland and uninteresting, though still nutritious enough to keep someone alive. Or it could be fun, unusual, flavorful—and maybe better for you. Tomato sauce wasn't much without basil. She knew that a judicious use of herbs and spices would cut down the amount of salt her family used. Using imagination cut down on all sorts of problems (not just salt intake) before they became more serious. Imagination had certainly reduced the boredom in their lives, at the same time it had added a sense of ritual and celebration that helped make routine and everyday events meaningful. Using imagination had given all of them a sense of freedom and adventure that had been lacking in their family before. Problems became challenges when looked at with the eyes of imagination. They also saw where they had been frittering away their time—not just the children but she and Jack as well. They dispensed with the unnecessary activities of their lives, though it hadn't made their lives more serious. Unnecessary didn't mean frivolous. There was plenty of frivolity—a lot more, in fact, than when their energy had been sapped by the unnecessary and unimportant. Take bickering, for example.

That had certainly expended a lot of energy for John and Laura. Some days they quarreled from the time they got up to the time they went to bed: who got the biggest piece of toast or the largest orange for breakfast, whose bed was made better or faster; which game should they play and whose toys should they use; which one was cheating; who had broken what favorite belonging; who had spilled the milk; and, of course, who started the argument. Their competition probably wasn't any worse than any other two children, but to Susan it seemed as though her children had invented the words *sibling rivalry*. She decided to use a different approach than punishment: She gave them each something imaginative to do—separately. That was the key. She isolated them and gave each one a project. Sometimes it was reviewing a chapter in social studies or some math problems or a science project. Or she gave each one a book to read and asked them to list all the words they didn't know, look them up, and define them. Or one of them had to practice a favorite piece on the piano. Occasionally she sat one of them down at the typewriter to write a story on a topic of her or his choosing or perhaps rewrite the end of a favorite book. If Jack was around to supervise, one of them might go to the garage to work on a building project.

Whatever the choices, they were all things John and Laura more or less enjoyed doing. Of course, if the quarrel had been particularly fierce, Susan might make each of them take a part of the house and clean it. Cleaning, she had found, was a good way of productively working off excess hostility and energy. She and Jack allowed no discussions about the squabble, not even what it was about, and certainly not whose fault it was. This resulted in the kids learning to resolve their quarrels before they intensified and brought either their mother or father into the room. (The rule for separation was that it had to be a loud, sustained, and intensifying quarrel; they did need to learn how to resolve conflicts for themselves.) What really surprised Susan was that after a few weeks with this rule in place, the kids would voluntarily stop playing together if they couldn't resolve their differences. She and Jack didn't need to think up alternative activities; the kids did it for themselves.

The point of imagination, Susan decided, was really to try to look at a situation or event from a different angle, to let light fall on a problem from a different direction. She began to see connections where she had never thought any existed. She recognized the extraordinary in the ordinary and vice versa. The world seemed more unified, more of a whole. Of course she believed that God created the universe, but at times life had seemed such a jumble that it was hard to see the hand of the

Creator in it—whether she was looking at nature or her neighborhood. She also began to understand a little why people wanted to know what made the universe hang together, what the stars meant, what were the laws that God had inserted at creation to insure that the earth moved on its axis in its orbit around the sun. As her imagination expanded to meet the challenges of her family and immediate surroundings, her interests broadened to more than just her family, almost without her being aware of it. An intellectual curiosity took hold of her and pushed her reading well outside its normal channels. Susan supposed that she was experiencing what had never happened to her during her school years. She didn't want her children to miss it, a love of learning and discovery and exploration. In a way she had become a little child again. Whether it was because Susan's imaginative explosion was so great or whether the children, too, were experiencing their own quiet revolution, Susan didn't know. But it was exciting.

Not only was her family's interest in learning about the world heightened, but as they learned, their awe as to what God had accomplished also increased. They became more worshipful on Sundays and this was sustained throughout the week. They worked together as a family on special projects—studying the stars or reading the biographies of people whose discoveries changed the way we live and think. In order to decide the issues for themselves, they confronted the works of Darwin and others whom their church and fellow Christians feared and distrusted.

The family discussions at mealtimes, though they had always been pretty lively, increased as they read and studied. The children had a greater sense of words and a curiosity about nuances and shades of meaning that hadn't existed before: they loved to think up verbs that were synonyms for the word *eating,* but all synonyms had to begin with the same letter as their main course: *c* for chicken, *f* for fish, *d* for duck, and so forth. That game increased their interest in the origins of words. If they didn't know the meaning of the word, Susan and Jack would explain it, Jack telling them the etymology and some of the other words that came from the same root. There was another benefit to such stimulating dinner conversation; the kids were so busy thinking up words that they ate their meals with little fuss or argument, even if it was something new or something they didn't think they liked. If they did notice, they showed greater interest and open-mindedness when Susan explained how the food was prepared and what herbs or spices had been used. It became a challenge for them to figure out where the different tastes originated. In the past, meals had often been unpleasant or tense.

Susan didn't know where her family's imagination would take them—to what new hobbies, subjects, or people to explore. Although she knew she would never become famous or rich because she used her imagination—she wasn't Rubenstein, after all—she knew that using her imagination had made a tremendous impact on the way she and her family lived. And for Susan and Jack, that was what they had wanted when they chose to limit television for reading and thinking and doing things together. They weren't trying to grow artists or scientists, just ordinary, contented people who saw their place and why God had put them in it. They wanted to show the grace of God at work in all the small parts of life.

For Susan, her family's ongoing experiment was having another exciting result. Jeanne was starting to use her imagination—a little less television, a few more books, a great deal more family interaction and discovery. Jeanne wasn't going to give up orange-striped walls—and really why should she, thought Susan—but she was exchanging what made her life tedious for something that made her see life as the divine gift it is.

Believing Impossible Things

Ordinary people such as you and I and Susan may have trouble breaking patterns and habits that stultify us. At times our imagination seems surrounded by rubbery globules of fat; we lack the mental detergent to dissolve the grease. Nor do we give our imagination time to stir up some suds. We suffer from Alice's affliction. We refuse to entertain the impossible, an activity not meant for us ordinary people, but for scientists or novelists.

If such people as Newton, Einstein, or Galileo did not need proof to believe what seemed impossible, the rest of us all fall short; yet they are exceptions even among scientists. Most scientists, no matter how brilliant, are like the rest of us: conservative, suspicious of anything new, unwilling to believe something for which there is no proof. If it seems impossible, they won't believe it. (Probably the difference between scientists and the rest of us is that their level of impossible is far greater. To some of us, turning off the television or getting our children to read is our level of impossible. Perhaps to a scientist it is to discover that a deeply believed principle, such as that the sun revolves around the earth, is wrong.)

Lewis Carroll in *Through the Looking Glass* talks about this problem. The White Queen is speaking to Alice.

"I can't believe that," said Alice.

"Can't you?" the Queen said, in a pitying tone. "Try again: draw a long breath and shut your eyes."

Alice laughed. "There's no use trying," she said: "one *can't* believe impossible things."

"I daresay you haven't had much practice," said the Queen. "When I was your age, I always did it for half-an-hour a day. Why, sometimes I've believed as many as six impossible things before breakfast."

Most of us haven't had any more practice than Alice in believing impossible things. Nor are we much interested. Belief is hard to come by even with the most possible of things to believe. Jesus probably wished that his disciples had practiced believing the impossible a little more often. His prediction that he would rise from the dead in three days seemed impossible. No one had ever done it. Despite how many times we read Paul's writings or the gospels, though, we persist in only believing what seems possible to us, forgetting that God is the author of the impossible—which may be the reason scientists have had so much trouble discovering the truth.

Louise B. Young in *The Blue Planet*, a beautiful book she calls "a journey of discovery," believes that scientists "are more reluctant than the average person to accept enthusiastically a radical, new idea (contrary to popular opinion). It is the business of science to explain how things occur that appear to be impossible. The feat requires imagination and independence of thought, attributes that are rare in any calling."[1] Young is talking about a way of seeing, the way Susan discovered in her simple family experiments. Imaginative people are not bothered by the accepted way of looking at or thinking about something. They ask the why-not or what-if questions, just as Jesus did. Independent thought, though, is difficult to sustain. The we've-never-done-it-that way people are the masters of ceremony. The rest of us may see a better way, but we seldom get a chance to prove we're right. Young wonders how much wasted time in scientific research has been the result of "conservatism of thought." The question could be enlarged to include any number of fields. "The truth," she writes, "usually proves to be more astonishing than the most radical hypothesis. Perhaps all young scientists should be assigned the exercise recommended by the White Queen—to practice believing impossible things for half-an-hour before breakfast."[2] So should we. If nothing else came of it, for scientists and the rest of us, our appetites and digestions would probably be better off.

Although the general populace probably doesn't know it, most great—and not so great—scientific discoveries were simply the products of intensely active imaginations. Often, imagination turns a mistake into a success. Imagination works two ways. It helps a person see an idea whole and know that it is the right idea. It also helps a person recognize that something can be made of a mistake. The history of science is filled with such examples—of vaccines being discovered, bacteria isolated, and so forth—merely as the result of error. In trying to discover one thing, scientists make another, often better, discovery. Lewis Thomas in *The Medusa and the Snail* praises imagination that takes error and makes it right (though he doesn't use the word *imagination,* that's what he's talking about). "Mistakes," he writes, "are at the very base of human thought, embedded there, feeding the structure like root nodules. . . . A good laboratory . . . has to run like a computer. . . . The days go by. And then, if it is a lucky day, and a lucky laboratory, somebody makes a mistake. . . . and then the action can begin. . . . The misreading is not the important error; it opens the way. The next step is the crucial one. If the investigator can bring himself to say, 'But even so, look at that!' then the new finding, whatever it is, is ready for snatching."[3] That's something like what God did for us in the Garden of Eden. When our ancestors blew it, God immediately saw the possibilities of a new discovery. It meant a lot of sacrifice and hard work on his part and ours—but it was worth it.

Clever industrial inventions, too, have a way of coming from aborted projects. Post-it Notes, those marvelous, ubiquitous little yellow notes from 3M with just a strip of adhesive at the top (my editor filled my manuscript with them), resulted from a failure. Researchers at 3M were trying to invent a new, stronger glue. The formula flopped. But one of the researchers said, "But even so, look at that": Post-it Notes and a financial success for 3M.

The person who invented Post-it Notes looked at his work with a cocked eye and a raised eyebrow. He also showed a quality common to many imaginative people—persistence; persistence to stay with an idea until it is exhausted. Imaginative people recognize the value of any and all ideas—not that at a given moment all ideas will be equally valuable or appropriate. But in another context—as with weak glue—the idea might be just exactly right. Many writers for just that reason keep journals or diaries, some place in which to jot down the odd idea or flash that comes when least expected. It could be the start of a new story or a wrinkle in the one a writer currently is working on. Imagination never sleeps. If imagination is a primary ingredient in what you do—and it should be for everyone—you should never lack ideas. A person may starve his imagination, or let it atrophy from lack of use; but if you feed and exercise it, imagination should not go stale.

Imagination is a state of being, a habit of the mind. There are writers who always seem to be in the state of writing. Not that they are always working, but imaginatively they are always creating something with words. Thus when the time for the physical labor comes, there is little breastbeating and agonizing. Imagination leads the fingers. Chaim Potok told me, in dis·cussing whether the life of an artist requires isolation, "You function inside the world, but you float inside an ambiance you create for yourself. . . . When I say that the artist isolates himself, I don't mean that he goes off to live on a desert island. There are parts of an artist that can sit and have a drink, and at the same time another part functions in a working way all the time as an artist."

Of course, this takes practice. Overnight a person can't develop this imaginative readiness, anymore than a person can overnight develop the habit of constant prayer. Both take the same kind of work, with obvious benefits. You reduce your warm-up time considerably; you might even be able to do away with it entirely. A singer or instrumentalist who practices regularly has less need to warm up before a performance than a person who practices occasionally. The same is true for imagination—or for prayer.

Meet Madeleine

Madeleine L'Engle is a good example of a writer who exercises her imagination, lives in a constant state of writing, and never neglects to feed her imagination. Whether traveling or at home, she is writing. In New York she writes in the library of the Cathedral of St. John the Divine, which is close to her upper west side apartment. On weekends she and her actor husband go to Crosswicks, and she writes on their farm in Connecticut.

Madeleine L'Engle's imagination has never been quiescent. She began to write when she was just a child, more out of self-defense, perhaps, than a love of words. She, like L. M. Montgomery's Emily, was different from other children. So she wrote—and read—to entertain herself, to keep herself from being too lonely. After college, though she continued to write, L'Engle worked as an actress, a member of a touring company. (It was here she met her husband.) Even while employed as an actress, her yellow pad was always with her; she wrote before the curtain went up, between acts, between scenes. She finally realized she was a writer not an actor and so with the expectant birth of her first child, she quit the theater. However, her understanding of the performing life—whether actor or concert pianist—fed her imagination and has resulted in some of her most poignant stories.

L'Engle was fortunate to have her first novel published quite quickly. Yet she knows too well that one published book is no guarantee that you'll ever get another one published. She wrote for more than ten years before she published another story. Looking back she realizes she was ahead of her time in children's books. *Meet the Austins* opens with a death. Children, she was told, should not read about death. Then she wrote a fantasy, *A Wrinkle in Time*, the book she is best known for (it won the Newberry in 1963). Children don't read fantasy, editors told her. Now, of course, she is one of the best-selling children's book authors in the world and in much demand as a speaker.

Ten years is a long time to exercise imagination without seeing any results—in a writer's case, nothing in print. During that time L'Engle wrote several unpublished books. She knew they were good; her imagination had been true, but she couldn't convince anyone else. She had committed her imagination and her books to God, but for a reason she couldn't understand, God was not allowing her to be published. On her fortieth birthday, she received another rejection, this one more difficult to take than the others because she had been so sure the publisher was ready to take the story. After her husband brought her the letter, she covered her typewriter and resolved never again to write. She was finally convinced: she was wrong, all the publishers right. But that night she awoke with her imagination writing another new story. She knew then that whether anyone ever read a word she wrote, she was a writer.

Unless you feed and exercise imagination, it will become stiff and unusable. How did she keep her imagination alive during that time? It was fed by her curiosity. Madeleine L'Engle has an insatiable curiosity about life—about nature, science, history, the macrocosmos as well as the microcosmos. You see the results of her curiosity on almost every page of her stories— from cultic men suffering from delusions to travel through time or space or mitochondria. She loves to read physics. Einstein and Eddington "opened up a world where I could conceive of a loving God who really could note the fall of every sparrow and count the hairs on every head." If anyone had ever told her that mathematics was a language, a philosophy (something she knows now because of her reading), she would have studied it intensely. No one did; she discovered science and math for herself. Once she read about the lives of a cell and mitochondria, she invented farandollae, so central to *A Wind in the Door*.

Because her imagination is fed, L'Engle is able to see things as they should be. She has been able to write of family life whole and rich, using the good and the bad from her own childhood as ingredients for her imaginative soup. In her Austin books, among others, she shows us how we ought to live. Without mentioning Christianity, she infuses her stories with a Christian world view. It comes to the reader as Christianity came to her, slowly, implicitly, irrevocably. The reader catches himself wondering why these people are different. Her characters are real, the work of her imagination. Not many of us know a mother who cooks supper on a bunsen burner (Meg and Charles Wallace's mother in the time trilogy); she is a good example of someone who lives imaginatively.

Madeleine L'Engle's books reflect her ideas, questions, curiosity. They show an incredible love of the Creator's mysterious handiwork that captivates us and will not let us go. There is a joyful sense of accepting the moment, of making the best of what we have, of spur-of-the-moment invention. Something may be unconventional—cooking stew on a bunsen burner— but if it works and eases the schedule, why not do it?

L'Engle, like the characters in her books, has a why-not attitude. She approaches ideas as possibilities. She sees life as a series of challenges that, in surmounting, will help make her the person God wants her to be. To accept life's challenges and mysteries as from his hand is a way of practicing the presence of God. Unlike so many people who see life as a series of obstacles to prevent them from having what they want, L'Engle looks at them as the zest of life. Her discovery as an adult of abstract mathematics and sophisticated scientific ideas has deepened her love of the mysteries of God's work and her faith in him. Her daily discoveries give her ideas for stories.

L'Engle doesn't live imaginatively because she is a writer. She is a writer because she lives imaginatively. We think that the profession must come first. Rather, the habit of imaginative living preceeds whatever profession a person chooses. When fed, her imagination has responded by creating stories for her. But it has also responded by giving her ideas as to what families should be like, how relationships should be formed, how to indicate respect for God's creatures, animal and human, as well as what stewardship means. L'Engle has a disciplined imagination. The ability to concentrate on what is important and distinguish important from unimportant requires a well-honed imagination. Madeleine L'Engle has that ability. She has sorted through the business of life and set her priorities. Anyone meeting her, visiting her home, listening to her speak or reading her books, quickly learns that she is a person whose imagination is elastic and supple enough to stretch as far and wide as it needs. If by nothing else, it is indicated by her love of children and her concern that their imaginations not be stunted somewhere mid grade school.

A Break from Tradition

Chaim Potok, like Madeleine L'Engle, knew early in his life that he wanted to write stories. But in the orthodox Jewish tradition, imagination is not highly prized, though the work of imagination in certain areas—telling stories and making music—is acceptable. Jewish history is rich in folklore and tales. But a life of imagination has never been an appropriate vocation for a strict Jew. In this century, though, we have seen Jews break from their traditions to become painters and writers (science, though it too demands great imagination, has been more acceptable). Chaim Potok understands these tensions well. He has written about them; he has lived them.

Potok was raised in a strict Jewish household. His days consisted of morning prayers, breakfast, attending his Jewish school to study Talmud and Bible and some "secular" subjects, returning home to eat, study, and go to bed only to repeat the process the next and every day but the Sabbath. The Jewish world Potok knew began and ended with Talmud; even studying the Bible was considered—at a certain level—frivolous and unimportant. But Potok had an imagination that would not be stifled. Some people need their imaginations awakened, but his was up and stirring before he knew it. He had an insatiable hunger and curiosity for stories, for art, for knowledge and understanding of people different from him and his family. Potok remembers well when a librarian thought he might enjoy reading the works of Evelyn Waugh (at the time he thought it was a woman writer who pronounced her name "wuff"); Waugh conquered him. He decided then that he wanted to give people a feeling of his tradition as real as Waugh had done for him, a Jew who knew no Gentiles, much less Irish Catholics. Potok remained in his Jewish schools, achieving the highest degrees his tradition offered; then he got a secular degree.

Potok's commitment to writing was great, perhaps made even greater by his other desire, which he knew would separate him forever from his people. He wanted to paint. Because the visual art forms are unquestionably anathema to orthodox Jews, he knew he would be ostracized. He concentrated all his imaginative energies into writing. Even so, Potok has been banned from some Jewish communities. He finds it ironic that he can speak to a conservative Christian college while he and his books are banned by yeshivas near his Philadelphia home. Potok chose to be a novelist, yet he nevertheless paints as an amateur; some of his paintings hang in his home in Philadelphia.

The characters in Potok's books—Reuven, Asher, and others—suffered too because their imaginations led them into unacceptable areas—to secular libraries, to text and higher criticism, to psychology, to paintings of nudes, and worst of all, to paintings of the crucifixion. For the Jewish tradition out of which Potok comes, to study and associate with secularism of any kind—by which Jews mean Christian thinkers as well as humanists—is to become unclean. It is like touching the dead. Religious Jews believe that imaginative curiosity will always lead to secularism. They still fight the battle that they did when Christ touched the dead and violated the Sabbath. Potok feels an affinity with conservative Christians at this point for they, also, distrust the imagination. In biblical studies, great curiosity and too many questions, they warn, will lead to textual and higher criticism. Although conservative Christians don't object to crucifixions, they strenuously object to nudes. We still trust the adage that curiosity killed the cat. Why-not and what-if questions may sound like theological doubt. Unusual metaphors about theology disturb some people and mark the user as suspect.

Both Potok and L'Engle have suffered because of their desire to write, L'Engle because her books were rejected for so many years, Potok because his works have been rejected by his own people. Both of them have turned their innate curiosity into food for their imaginations. With Potok, it has been a model of how to tell the story of his people. With L'Engle it has become the subjects of her stories. Potok's focus has been much narrower than L'Engle's but the way they read and explore ideas and people outside themselves has been much the same.

Curiosity. Intrigued by new ideas. A simple appreciation for life coupled with an educated understanding of its simplicity. A passion for what-if and why-not questions. These characteristics mark L'Engle and Potok. They mark nearly every example of a person living imaginatively, Christian or non-Christian, God's common grace at work.

Chapter 6, Notes

1. Louise B. Young, *The Blue Planet* (Boston: Little, Brown & Co., 1984), p. 67.

2. Ibid., p. 68.

3. Lewis Thomas, *The Medusa and the Snail* (Bantam, 1980), pp. 30, 31.

Chapter 7

Physics Melted in His Mouth

Imagination, as the *imago Dei*, existed before the Fall. Without it, Adam could not have named the animals, nor could he have cared for the earth. Perhaps it was imagination out of control that drove Eve and Adam to sin—a curiosity to know more than they did at that moment, though a curiosity controlled more by hubris than imagination.

Curiosity, whether or not it is disciplined, is a powerful spur to the imagination. Such novelists as Potok have it in abundance. He asks, What would happen if I put this character in this situation? What would he do? What would the people around him do? What if he faced this temptation or that? Wouldn't it be interesting to find out? When a novelist becomes intrigued with the possibilities, with the characters he is creating, he must write. Imagination and curiosity walk together.

It does take great imagination to break from long-held beliefs—to know which are the right questions to ask, and then to recognize you have the right answers. Scientists as well as novelists ask the I-wonder-what-would-happen-if questions. Good scientists have an unerring ability to ask the right questions; great scientists the fundamental ones. The scientists who changed our concepts of reality have had the greatest imaginations and have asked the most exacting what-if questions, men like Newton in an earlier century and Einstein in ours.

Imagination's Influence on the Sciences

It may be said that for the eighteenth and nineteenth centuries, and even for the early twentieth century, the arts dominated the life of imagination. But in the closing days of this century, the sciences now inform the imaginations of artists and ordinary people. Science provides the metaphors, the images, and the aesthetic atmosphere of our society. (As we have seen, L'Engle has been greatly influenced by science and such books as *The Limitations of Science*, Potok very little.) Scientists look for beauty in their experiments, mathematicians for element and form in their theorems. Moreover, since it is impossible to observe the microworld without changing it, theories now held by most physicists are the result of imagining what occurs in the microworld rather than by observing what occurs.

The great discoveries in mathematics and science have resulted because someone was able to answer the what-if questions better than someone else. Many solutions come not through long days, months, or years of journeyman research, but through metaphors that occur to them at odd times of the day or night. Not that scientists don't work in the most indefatigable way. But in instance after instance, the answers came when the work was put aside and their rational minds were occupied with other matters. Then, it seems, their imaginations could function unencumbered—though the digging had to come first.

Alan Wolf in *Taking the Quantum Leap* credits imagination with developing quantum mechanics, a theory of how the universe behaves. Another physics professor, largely influenced by Owen Barfield's book *Saving the Appearances: A Study in Idolatry*, has written *Physics As Metaphor*, in which he defines science as a poetic activity. Physical scientists, he says, are trying to understand the meaning of life, just as philosophers and artists do. Their tools are not any different: metaphors, images, symbols—the works of imagination. There is no denying that some of the best and most beautiful writing today is coming not from poets or novelists but from scientists (among nonfiction book sales science writing is on the increase). People are fascinated not just by the facts, but by the beauty of the writing and the metaphors that, though scientific, are still universal. The metaphors can teach us about ourselves: about how to live, about relationships, about what life itself means.

When people say science is a religion, they have said more than they realize. It is intended as a comment on the commitment that science draws from its professionals or from those who look to science as a god; it is a statement hinting at idolatry. But it is also a statement that science is dealing with cosmological or theological questions (technology, which is separate from science, deals with solutions to practical problems, and the two should not be linked together). It would not be unfair to say that science today is an art.

If people question that science is not necessarily based on observation or fact but on ideas and metaphors, we only need look at evolution. This theory transformed the way society thought about humanity without the slightest evidence that evolution could happen or ever has. As with the idea that there were once fairies in England, it is no more than an interesting notion. Yet, Darwin's idea captured the public imagination and has stuck there, immovable, ever since. It's theological ramifications have been far reaching. The power of certain ideas to become metaphors almost guarantees their public acceptance. People are hungry for stimulating images that help explain themselves to themselves. Computers, for example, have become an irresistible and controlling metaphor for how the human brain functions; it has reopened the question of the mind/body split. People who developed computers and their programs showed great imagination, yet verge on relinquishing their imaginations to the machine.

An Uncollared Imagination

People as well as objects can become an image of an age, though it does not happen often. Yet certainly this is true of

Einstein. We know his face—his elderly face, that is. It has been painted, acted, made up, and trivialized in a way that only the advertising imagination could have accomplished. Nearly every science magazine has run advertisements that feature Einstein for some specious philosophical or occult book or tape. On television he advertises computers or stereo components. (We will be seeing less of Einstein in the future, if the executors of his estate have their way.) The myth surrounding the man is almost greater than the truth. Einstein, himself, would have been totally uninterested in any of the products.

Einstein's life was one of great contradictions. Although a pacifist, in his elder years he worked for Zionism and helped create the bomb. Most of the work for which he became famous was finished early in his life—accomplished in approximately a year—and he spent the rest of his life active in world politics and waiting for his theories to be validated through others' experiments. (Not that he greatly cared whether his theories were proved true, as they subsequently were; he knew he was right.) He became known as a philosopher-scientist, and unlike Newton who hated to publish and had no compulsion to explain how he had arrived at his ideas, Einstein wrote, explained, taught, and occasionally gave interviews. He and the mathematician Henri Poincaré have provided us with knowledge as to how the scientific imagination works.

Einstein was born in Germany, a country he hated all his life; as a young adult he renounced his German citizenship to become Swiss. Contrary to the myth that he was a poor student, flunking mathematics, he always did well, particularly in mathematics and physics. It is true his teachers disliked him, seeing nothing of promise or exception in him. This continued well into his advanced studies. Einstein disliked the gymnasium educational system because of its rigid discipline and overbearing authoritarianism; all his life he had difficulty with authority. Despite that, he learned self-discipline and self-control; the gymnasium taught him how to concentrate and reinforced his natural singlemindedness. Without these characteristics

Einstein would never have persevered with his special theory of relativity.

A Jewish medical student introduced Einstein to physics and mathematics when he was twelve. He read two standard works of the time on the subjects and was soon studying higher mathematics on his own. By the time he was thirteen he was also reading Kant—not exactly the fare of an average child.

Einstein's education was erratic; his parents moved frequently. When Einstein was sixteen, at his father's insistence, he went to Zurich to study at the Swiss Federal Polytechnic School or ETH (the abbreviation of its German name). However, he failed the entrance exam. Because of his exceptional understanding of mathematics, the principal of the school arranged for Einstein to study for a year in another school so that he could pass the entrance exam—which he did. His experience at the ETH was not a great deal different from his earlier schooling; he angered and offended his teachers by his arrogance. In particular he angered his physics teacher, and after graduation the school declined to offer him the customary low teaching position. Although there was a physics position open, rather than hire Einstein the professor chose someone from outside the field.

Eventually he found a job with the patent office in Switzerland. During his years there he developed the theories for which he became famous. The patent office gave him enough income to live on. It also provided his imagination with the time and space he needed to work out his theories. While his conscious, reasoning mind worked on patents, his imagination worked on physics.

Einstein thought and taught in metaphors, as when he thought of himself being in a free-falling elevator and connected it to the theory of relativity. He knew that without an unusually active imagination he would never have achieved the shattering successes that he did. His mother insisted on music lessons; Einstein became quite a good amateur violinist and music meant much to him throughout his life, enhancing his ability to be a metaphor-maker. His Uncle Jakob also taught him early the

value of metaphorical thinking. " 'Algebra is a merry science,' "
Uncle Jakob would say. 'We go hunting for a little animal
whose name we don't know, so we call it *x*. When we bag our
game we pounce on it and give it its right name . . . ' In many
of Einstein's later attempts to present the theory of relativity to
mathematicians, there is recourse to something not so very different; to analogies with elevators, trains, and ships."[1] Einstein
had the inquisitive nature of a child. He said that because his
intellectual development was arrested, he never thought about
space and time until he became an adult. Normally a child wonders about such things, but lacks the mathematical or scientific
tools to analyze them. By the time Einstein wondered about
space and time, he had the tools. Despite his education, which
normally removes as many vestiges of childlike imagination as
possible, Einstein retained many. Wanting to understand the
harmony in the universe, he was interested only with essentials,
not peripherals. His work at the patent office had another advantage: it forced him to hone his critical and analytical skills.

In 1905 Einstein published three papers in a physics journal, one of which was on the theory of relativity. It was clear,
precise, and lacking the bugaboo of academic writing—foot-
notes and long quotations from other sources. Einstein, following the path others had begun—Newton, for instance—was on
his own. He had no connection with a university or other scientists. He worked alone in his room, thinking about the funda-
mentals. Einstein was twenty-six. A vague idea of relativity had
first occurred to him when he was sixteen, but for the next seven
years he lived with them incessantly. Once the idea became
clear to him, it was only a matter of a few weeks to write his
theory down. The other papers, one on Brownian motion and
the other known as Einstein's "photoelectric paper," also repre-
sented great imagination. The latter brought him the Nobel
Prize in physics in 1921. (The Nobel committee had a difficulty
in awarding him the physics prize; they couldn't give it to him
for relativity because the rules stated it had to be for something
that had proved beneficial to mankind in some way. People still
weren't certain that relativity was true, much less that they had

found a practical application for it, whereas his photoelectric theory had already proven it's practical worth.) The paper was pivotal in the further development of quantum mechanics, with which he vehemently disagreed and which isolated him in later life from the center of scientific life. (It is ironic that he ended his intellectual life in as much isolation as he began it.) He could never reconcile what he reported in that paper, a seeming duality in nature with his view of God. He firmly believed in the harmony and balance of the Creator's mind and methods.

Einstein's drive to understand the harmony of the universe helped him persist with his theory of relativity for years, though he was at times confused and disheartened. His belief in a Creator who made the universe whole and balanced also helped. Einstein was a theoretical physicist. He dealt with ideas and imagination, not with observation. He thought up the answers to the questions he posed for himself; it was the responsibility of others to provide the physical evidence that he was right. As a colleague said in trying to secure a teaching position for him, the job of a theoretical physicist is to ask the right questions. Einstein took ideas that had been apparent to many scientists and connected them. It wasn't the difficulty that so much astounded scientists about Einstein's theories; it was their great simplicity.

Einstein knew that imagination had played a significant role in his discoveries. We might say he tried to approach the universe using God's eyes, to see creation as God sees it. "Einstein himself was always ready to agree that inventiveness, imagination, the intuitive approach—the very stuff of which artists rather than scientists are usually thought to be made—played a serious part in his work. And when his friend Janos Plesch commented years later that there seemed to be some connection between mathematics and fiction, a field in which the writer made a world out of invented characters and situations and then compared it with the existing world, Einstein replied: 'There may be something in what you say. When I examine myself and my methods of thought, I come to the conclusion that the gift of fantasy has meant more to me than my talent for absorbing positive knowledge.'"[2] He needed an extraordinary ability and desire to ask the what-if and why-not questions before his knowledge of mathematics or science ever came into play. Einstein allowed his imagination to roam as wide and as long as it wanted. He never collared it or said in his early years, "This can't be right." Rather he said, "Let's see if this might be right," no matter how strange or far-fetched the idea.

For some reason this inventive and playful imagination is the world of the young scientist, not the old. Einstein made his three great discoveries in the same year. (Of course, we can't discount the years of thought that went into his conclusions and from which his papers were written.) Perhaps in truly revolutionary discoveries a person must spend a lifetime thereafter explaining and teaching what he has learned. During Einstein's middle years someone commented on the electricity of his teaching by saying that physics melted in his mouth: This man loved his work.

Greater Than Einstein

Newton, too, had astounded the scientists of his day. Because the law of gravity is embedded into us from early school days, we cannot appreciate how revolutionary the idea was. A falling apple was a common occurrence; everyone knew they fell from trees; but only Newton connected the fall of the apple and the fact that the moon stayed in its orbit. Newton was the one to develop "the first modern synthesis of the physical world, a logical explanation of the universe."[3] As great as was Einstein's achievement, greater still was Newton's. Einstein merely built a room onto the edifice Newton had designed and constructed.

Newton made his great discoveries also in just a year of his life, and at a young age. In 1666 he had to leave Cambridge because of the plague; he was twenty-four when he escaped to his home in Lincolnshire. That summer he developed three startling ideas that revolutionized mathematics and science. He developed the calculus, the law of gravity, and Newton's laws of motion. When asked in later life how he made three such startling discoveries, he replied, simply, "By always thinking about them." He believed that his intellectual and imaginative powers were then at their height.

Newton worked in virtual isolation. He had no colleagues with whom he could argue, raise questions, test his ideas. The test had to come from within himself; his imagination had to serve as both inventor and skeptic with no one to satisfy but himself. He claimed merely to be following the same road laid down centuries earlier; he merely "stood on the shoulders of giants." Because Newton talked little about his discoveries or how he made them, we cannot say definitely that mental images, metaphors, imaginative fantasy helped him make his great discoveries, but everything we know about how the scientific or artistic mind works would lead us to conclude that Newton was no different. When he thought about the orbit of the moon, an apple falling, or the motion of particles on earth, he must in some way have imagined how these disparate elements were connected. He, like Einstein, was looking for laws that would answer questions about the fundamental nature of the universe. It takes an extraordinarily strong imagination to understand that a falling apple is the answer to why the moon doesn't fall out of its orbit and crash into the earth. Newton started with as few preconceived notions as is humanly possible; he willingly increased the space that housed his imagination to find some answers. (When we realize that Newton anticipated quantum mechanics and the question as to whether light was a wave or a particle, we recognize his greatness.)

Balancing Two Worlds

As studies in how imagination works in a particular area and how radically it can change life, Einstein and Newton are ultimate examples. However, as models for good imaginative relationships, they aren't particularly exemplary. Einstein did not like people; they annoyed and interfered with him. His first marriage failed, his second, to his cousin Elsa, lasted because she knew her role in Einstein's life and never pretended to understand—even a little—his scientific achievements (his first wife had been a physicist, too). Elsa protected him from the public, sheltered him, cared for him, entertained his colleagues. He made the decisions, she carried them out. She spared him much that ordinary people deal with, so that he could devote his time to theoretical physics (though after those early years and later in 1919 when he developed the general theory of relativity from his special theory of relativity, he made no further startling discoveries). Newton, too, was a crusty character, though he never married.

Not all great inventive imaginations, of course, have abysmal relationships with those close to them; but many great men have had such miserable—or nonexistent—personal lives. We don't need to look just at great scientists and inventors; there are abundant examples among theologians and evangelists (witness Wesley) whose imaginations have led them, driven them night and day, in great service of God and humanity to the destruction of their immediate circle of family and friends. This cannot be blamed on the gift of imagination, but, as with Adam and Eve, on some hubris or "o're vaulting ambition" (as Milton described Satan in *Paradise Lost*) hidden from the person, but perfectly clear to those around him.

People need balance; they need a close circle of family and friends to serve as mirrors and guardians; imagination run rampant is no better in theology or science than it is in writing. Our imagination must be disciplined by God. Purple prose and an undisciplined catalog of metaphors is imagination out of control. So is the person whose imagination takes him into great intellectual or artistic adventures but leaves no energy for great personal adventures, where imagination, too, plays a crucial role. Nevertheless we must take imaginative models where we find them. Not everyone has the largeness of imagination to ask the right probing questions or recognize when he has the answer. We are probably fortunate that only a few people have such an intense imaginative drive for discovery. While recognizing that these models are flawed, we can still learn from them. Whether someone is inventing the integral calculus or pursuing a good marriage or raising children, the principles are the same. Einstein and Newton did not apply to their relationships the principles that governed their imaginative drive—but we can apply them to ours.

Ordinariness Transformed

One need not be an Einstein or a Newton to show imagination in ordinary ways every day. Yet each of us has something that melts in his mouth. Dr. Donald Hebb, one of the leading theoreticians on the human brain, says, "Every normal human being is creative all the time, thinking of new ways to make bread, new ways to serve breakfast, new ways to plant the garden. Creativity is not something that occurs only in the brain of outstanding individuals. It is a normal aspect of the human brain function. And it is accounted for by the almost infinite number of possibilities for new combinations of cell assemblies."[4] Although I would use the word *imaginative,* rather than *creative,* I agree. The potential for ordinary people to suddenly become well known for some particularly startling imaginative idea is great; it happens all the time. Yet, we're always surprised when we hear about women and men who have started successful businesses, for example, based on simple, yet clever ideas: imagination at work. Often the people involved are as surprised as everybody else. This happens quite often with writers. Unprepossessing people often turn out to be quite amazing characters. (I'm talking, of course, as though there are such people as "ordinary," which I don't for an instant believe, though I do believe there are people who *think* themselves ordinary.)

Two children's book authors, quite ordinary in themselves, have created quite extraordinary characters that will live long after their creators have died. P. L. Travers may not be familiar to everyone, but Mary Poppins certainly is. During the thirties, while Travers was recovering from an illness (an important point, as we will discover), Mary Poppins arrived. Travers refuses to say she invented, imagined, or created her (as with Lewis and Tolkien, she doesn't believe people create anything; we merely use imagination to restir the pot God put on simmer). As she does in the first book, Mary Poppins simply showed up one day. And once she was there she had to do something; Mary Poppins is not one to sit around doing nothing. As a servant—Travers sees herself as well as Mary Poppins as servants—Travers knew what the prim Miss Poppins would do. She explained in *The Junior Book of Authors*: "I have always thought Mary Poppins came then solely to amuse me and that it was not till a friend saw some of her adventures written down and thought them interesting that she decided to stay long enough for me to put her into a book. I never for one moment believed that I invented her. Perhaps she invented me, and that is why I find it so difficult to write autobiographical notes!"[5] Mary Poppins is a connector. She sees the world as a whole, balanced—the every day and the holiday all fitting together harmoniously. That is Travers's view, too.

Mary Poppins is a governess, serving the Banks family, a rather ordinary, middle-class British family. The parents, as in many British children's stories (E. Nesbitt, for example, or C. S. Lewis) are either missing or inconsequential: The children hold center stage. Also, Travers is writing fairy stories, myths fallen into space and time; she has just disguised it better. Few people think of fairy tales when they think of Mary Poppins. But like Aslan or the Phoenix (in *The Phoenix and the Carpet* by E. Nesbitt), Mary Poppins is the fairy tale come true, the overwhelming wish of every imaginative child, when what-if and if-only questions are dreamed about with a breathless awe and longing. At a certain level children do believe that Mary Poppins can come to *them* on the wind, out of the sky, without hair mussed or clothes awry. Children—and lots of adults, if the truth be known—believe that if they could only find a wardrobe, they, too, could find Narnia and Aslan or that an old rug is really a magic flying carpet holding a phoenix and marvelous adventures that don't include eating spinach or making their bed. Don't we wish we could have such adventures, too? Don't we wish the stories were true?

P. L. Travers, C. S. Lewis, and others wrote stories that they wanted to read. Travers found Mary Poppins irresistible, an enigma, a strange contradiction that sums up a lot of life—

for adults as well as for children. Yet, she is always and only HERSELF (somehow that needs capital letters). Mary Poppins expands a child's imagination. Travers believes that you have to love the stories for themselves before the stories will yield up their secrets. If any story can make children—and adults wise enough to read or reread them—love the stories for themselves, Mary Poppins can. My third grade teacher read us Mary Poppins—one or two, perhaps, but certainly not all of them— but we were enraptured. Life seemed luminescent while reading about her, and I proceeded to read the rest of them on my own.

The stories' simplicity is part of the charm. Quite compli-cated and unexplainable things happen, but all in such a simple, nonchalant, everyday way that the magic and mystery are heightened. The stories are images of grace; they describe how God's adventures appear, as well as Mary Poppins's. Of her-self, P. L. Travers says, "I'm not a scholar or a teacher. I'm not anything very much. I'm just somebody who remembers and links things up. Things link themselves within me."[6] In a sense, that's what the gospel writers were, people who remembered things and linked them up. That is also what real theology should be—connections and remembrances for people who have never known or who have forgotten more than they knew, as in the yearly reenactment of Passover or those Christians who mark Maundy Thursday with Seder. Travers's imagination makes the connections; through her imagination ideas, paradoxes, conundrums, or contradictions stick to her ribs and become part of her physical being so that without them she is no longer herself. Certainly the Mary Poppins books have provided rib-sticking food for many children.

Yet, and here again she is one with Lewis, she never in-tended to write solely for children. It is a great misfortune that most of the strikingly imaginative stories in our culture are now reserved and marketed only to children. Not that children don't need or deserve such books; it's that adults need them so much more (science fiction is an exception, but most sci-fi is not imaginative the way that I mean it; the atmosphere's all wrong). Travers says in an essay, "I Never Wrote for Children," "You do not chop off a section of your imaginative substance and make a book specifically for children for—if you are honest—you have, in fact, no idea where childhood ends and maturity begins. It is all endless and all one."[7] Again we hear Christ's words, "Unless you become as little children." It's a lesson we still have not understood, much less mastered. Travers points out that the Middle English meaning of *understand* is literally to stand under. Not many of us stand under Christ's words. Not many of us would stand for becoming children again, much less stand under the notion of childness. Christ's words should be the roof over our heads; only in that sense can we talk about being sheltered from the storm.

Inactivity, a Productive Stimulus

In this shelter, there is silence. A common characteristic of all the imaginative people we have looked at is their need for silence, almost for emptiness. Einstein and Newton worked in isolation; L'Engle writes alone in a cathedral library, Potok in a quiet room in his house when his family is gone or in an apartment in Tel Aviv. Travers first wrote *Mary Poppins* while sick in bed. Astrid Lindgren, too, found silence a productive stimulus for her imagination. She is another ordinary person who discovered a quite extraordinary and by now legendary character, Pippi Longstocking.

Just as Mary Poppins found P. L. Travers, wacky, red-haired, pig-tailed Pippi Longstocking found Astrid Lindgren. Lindgren's daughter—a hard-to-entertain patient—was ill with pneumonia. One evening when her daughter was nagging, "Tell me something" and, exhausted, Lindgren asked, "Tell you what?" out came, "Tell me about Pippi Longstocking." There she was, and anyone with such a strange name had to be a strange character.

There it probably would have ended, but Lindgren fell on a patch of ice, spraining both ankles. She was forced to stay in bed for awhile—remember Travers—and to pass the time she wrote down Pippi Longstocking stories in shorthand. That is still the way Lindgren writes today, shorthand first. Because her body was confined, just as was Travers's, her imagination had to keep things moving.

Sometimes physical mobility and the everyday busyness of living can get in the way of a strong imagination. A person doesn't see the need for using imagination; he's using his hands and feet instead. The space is being used for physical activity with no room left for imagination to run and jump. Lindgren was just a mother (the word *just* is not meant pejoratively). Pippi Longstocking was an out-of-patience mother's last-ditch stand to keep a fretful child amused. There isn't a mother around who doesn't understand the situation out of which Pippi was born. Lindgren says, "So maybe every children's book author should be sick in bed for a while. And when I write, I lie in bed, put the book down in shorthand, and I have the feeling that nothing outside exists, I'm just on my bed in my little room and I can go and meet the people I want to."[8]

Getting her books published was as much of a fluke as writing about Pippi in the first place. Three years after the first storytelling, she decided to write out and give her daughter the Pippi story as a birthday present. Since she was copying it anyway, she decided to send it to a publisher—with an apologetic note which said that she was upset with the unusual things Pippi did. She never expected the publisher to take the book—he didn't. In the meantime she had written another story for a publisher's contest. She won second prize. The next year Lindgren sent in Pippi and won first prize.

Lindgren's books have been translated into more than twenty-five languages, evidence that children love to read stories that stretch and stir their imaginations. In the midst of technology that deadens imagination, stories like Lindgren's provide a needed antidote. The author complains that she can no longer write for today's teenagers; they are so different from how she grew up and what she knew. "When I was a child," she says, "we didn't have cars, TV, radio, or even many films. So there was a lot of room for imagination!"[9] Although she may be right about teenagers today, their need for imaginative literature is greater than ever. Their rooms have been crowded with anti-imagination devices, which even they eventually find boring. It may take awhile for them to recover, though such writers as Lindgren or L'Engle can speed the healing.

Lindgren notes that children no longer play like children once did. In fact, they don't seem to know how. As a child, she and her siblings enacted whatever their imaginations thought up. They also had lots of ideas from the books they read. A playmate a little older than Lindgren introduced her to the world of fairy stories, and she was never the same. She still remembers the day and room where she met fairies—the kitchen of a poor farmhand. Although she never intended to write, when she was flat in bed with nothing to do, it seemed a natural thing.

The Senses Trigger Imagination

As we saw in chapter three, imagination and memory are strongly linked. Some philosophers and psychologists believe that imagination is impossible without memory, or that imagination makes memory possible. What no one knows, of course, is how either works. Sight certainly has something to do with it. Researchers have recently studied Einstein's brain tissue to see if it is different from the average male brain. It is, but only significantly so in the area of vision. We also know that memory and imagination are triggered as much by smell as by sight (probably even more so). Much of L'Engle's writing, characters, and philosophy relates to the smell of things—people, situations. Lindgren fell in love with books after she heard a fairy tale. Then she started buying them: "Imagine, to be the sole owner of a book—a wonder I didn't faint for pure happiness! I can still remember how these books smelled when they arrived, fresh from the printer; yes, I started by smelling them, and there was no lovelier scent in all the world. It was full of foretaste and anticipation."[10] Maurice Sendak, the famous illustrator and children's book author (*Where the Wild Things Are*, among others), too, smelled books as a child. So did I. Even today I smell the books I read; it tells me something about what's to come. It excites my imagination to anticipate a treat, just as much as wonderful cooking smells tell me something good is in the oven. My husband enjoyed philosophy in graduate school because his textbook smelled good enough to eat. For people who live imaginative lives, all the senses are important. Whether sight or smell or sound or touch predominates is unimportant. C. S. Lewis saw pictures, perhaps the way Einstein or Newton saw pictures of the universe. The job of a writer, Lewis explained, is to connect all the pictures together; that's where the work comes in.

Imprisoned but Not Confined

Imaginative people live in at least two kinds of space, that in which gravity confines them and unlimited imaginative space. It seems as if the greater the physical confinement the larger the imaginative space grows. John Bunyan and Alexander Solzhenitsyn are two examples. *Pilgrim's Progress* was written in prison, a tremendous feat. Greater still was that of Solzhenitsyn, who wrote in prison despite the fact that he was allowed no paper. He wrote in his head and memorized what he wrote as he wrote it. Only later did he write it down. Prison stripped him of everything except his imagination. Instead of destroying it, prison actually fed and strengthened his imagination. The gulag forced him to live a far greater and more meaningful life than he might have done had he had physical freedom and material comfort.

In a sense, we all are prisoners of our physical state, of "brother ass" as St. Francis called the body. This is not to denigrate the body, but to recognize that it limits our movement, strength, energy, space, and time. We cannot, no matter how great our desire, physically be in two places at once. It is our imaginations that enlarge our living space for us; we can be in two places at once—cleaning the house or mowing the lawn and yet visiting a friend or visiting the throne of grace. Such people as Einstein, Travers, or Solzhenitsyn had no greater opportunity to live in two kinds of space simultaneously than we do (though outer circumstances may have removed from them the choice of a free physical existence; even Einstein was confined to a narrow room and a narrow life by his inability to find an academic job). They were simply conscious that they lived in two worlds. Most of us are not. We take what we can see and touch and physically feel for our world, ignoring the soft scent and light touch of the other worlds we occupy.

People have made much of the idea of slowing down to smell the flowers; the idea has sent scores of people scampering like so many city mice back to the land. Yet the people who truly appreciate nature seem to have a greater sense of the imaginative world that can be glimpsed or visited through nature. Nature isn't the end, in other words; it's the means, a temporal vehicle or channel through which we see the eternal world. Sigurd Olson was one of our greatest nature writers. What made him so well-loved was not only his beautiful writing and his acute eyesight but also his intense understanding—in the Middle English sense—of the nature of nature. His essays are filled with spiritual insight and keen imaginative awareness of the values to which nature points. In *The Singing Wilderness* he sounds for the reader's inner ear the music of God, whether it be the crisp crunch of snow under boot or snowshoe, the swish of skiis, the slash of skates, the call of the migrating goose or the splash and swoosh of a trout well hooked and playing the line. All these reverberate against Olson's imaginative ear; and he experiences God's voice. C. S. Lewis experienced it too, but called it joy. Although his ear heard it under different circumstances, the music was the same.

Solzhenitsyn learned to bless prison. Looking back on his small apartment and repetitive job, Einstein was grateful, too, for his prison; he knew it allowed him the imaginative space he needed to work. Certainly Travers and Lindgren found grand company when they visited their other worlds. People need, if not the confinement of Bunyan or Solzhenitsyn or even the illness of Lindgren or Travers, to be aware of their confinements. We all have them, rich or poor. Listening to some people, we might assume that they are all too aware of their confinements: complaints, anger, bitterness, frustration, or worry rule these people. Yet they are only aware of the discomfort of prison, not its grace. They fail to grasp the great freedom they have to live another way in another world, refusing to look at the imaginative potential in even a limited and narrowly proscribed existence.

All of us know, or have heard of, people whose lives could not be any more limited, and still be called a life: people confined to a wheelchair who once were active and healthy, the elderly trapped by health or age or lack of money, people deaf or blind. When we see such people live joyously and giving joy to others, we are often astounded. How can they be that way? We point to them, make them models, envy them, shake our heads and say we could never be like that. That is no doubt true; most of us aren't that way with fewer limitations. Although we may occasionally sense it, we cannot see the strength of their imaginations to move beyond their physical existence to another plane and to reach out to others in prayer and love. Elizabeth Goudge in one of her novels has a main character who never leaves her bedroom. Her bed, her window, and back again to her bed—her world. Yet she knows, loves, and prays for all the other characters in the book. Her only real function in the plot is as touchstone and transition, a kind of confined omniscient voice; her purpose in the life of the story, to pray. As she uses every ounce of imaginative strength to keep herself to her God-appointed task, she is more strongly connected to those she loves than most of us who can easily see or call our loved ones.

Limitations—yours, mine—are good and not to be grumbled at. They are to be consecrated and given up to God—after all, what else, really, do we have to give him?—so that we can then concentrate on the other space we live in, where the limitations are not so great.

Chapter 7, Notes

1. Ronald W. Clark, *Einstein: The Life and Times* (World Publishing Company, 1971), p. 12.

2. Ibid., p. 74.

3. Ibid., p. 87.

4. Richard Restak, *The Brain* (Bantam, 1979), pp. 228-229.

5. Jonathan Cott, *Pipers at the Gates of Dawn: The Wisdom of Children's Literature* (Mcgraw Hill, 1985), p. 196.

6. Ibid., p. 202.

7. Ibid., p. 204.

8. Ibid., p. 147.

9. Ibid., p. 148.

10. Ibid., p. 152.

Chapter 8

Bewitching Business

The little boy was somewhat puzzled, now that he'd recovered from his surprise. He knew that the man in the ring was real. All his stories were real. It was just that none of them had ever stubbed his toes on the coffee table before. He felt sorry for the Knight. He'd never much liked the dumb furniture—always bumping him in soft places. But the Knight obviously wasn't used to normal household stuff. His castle probably had very little furniture, if it was anything like the pictures of other castles the little boy had seen.

Dendra sounded just the place where a person could have real adventures. The Witch would be absolutely thrilling, probably a real old crone, black hat and all.

"I suppose she can send him back there," thought the child. "If only there was a way I could see what happens to him once he's gone. I don't suppose I could go with him. Mother would get really mad. But she wouldn't mind it if I just watched. Sure'd be better than stinky old cartoons." Road Runner had never visited him in person.

All the time the little boy was thinking this—it took very little time, really, since he thought it all at once and not a sentence at a time, as I had to repeat it—the Knight stood there awkwardly, hoping and worrying and wondering what the Witch was up to. Finally, he said, "You *can* send me back, can't you?"

"Well," replied the girl, "I know I can return you to the ring. And since you're just a story I'm making up, I don't see why I can't send you back to wherever you say you came from. Dendra, was that it?"

"A ring? A story? What are you talking about?" shouted the Knight. "I'm the ruler—or I was—of Dendra. I . . ." Oh bother, he thought, it doesn't seem all that real any more. He was beginning to feel a little silly in a full suit of armor with these children dressed in almost nothing.

"I suppose you want to go along," the girl said to the child, who nodded his head enthusiastically. "You can't. But, you could look into the ring and watch what happens. The inside is a lot bigger than the outside of this ring. Just don't get too close or you might fall in. Then, of course, there's always your mind's eye." The little boy nodded again, in agreement.

"Then back he goes."

In a few moments, the Knight was once again flat. This time he didn't feel quite so alone. He knew that a little boy, at least, was watching him, sharing in his adventures.

"Ow! That felt like a thorn," he yelled aloud. Somehow a thorn had sneaked past his armor and rammed into his backside. Boy did it hurt.

Where was he? He opened his eyes and looked around. He was lying face up in a patch of brambles. That's all he could see—sky and brambles wherever he looked. "That meddling girl has sent me to the wrong place. I'll bet I look ridiculous."

Things were getting out of hand so far as the Knight was concerned. He'd always been a patient, plodding sort of fellow, but all this travel without benefit of horse was beginning to unseat his equilibrium. "Women. All because of women. What I wouldn't give for a sight of good old Gumples. Maybe he can pull this blasted thorn out with his teeth." The Knight was trying to get himself out of the brambles, but he was too heavy, a whole lot heavier than he had been a little while ago. He couldn't sit up or roll over. A person never knows when he is well-off. Being flat didn't look so bad to the Knight right now.

He stayed this way for some time. At first he tried to move, but every effort merely drove the thorn deeper. He could almost feel his flesh swelling and becoming infected. He supposed it was poisonous—bound to be, probably kill him off or drastically change his personality. He had just resigned himself to any one of a number of terrible futures or no future at all, when he heard a familiar sound. Suddenly he was nuzzled by a horse, a most sensible horse, his horse, Gumples. "So, I am back in Dendra."

And he was. The girl had done her best to return him to the exact place he had left. But, really, she was only a girl and not a witch. She had no way of knowing that in the time the Knight had been gone, the Witch had changed things a little. The lovely clearing where she and the Knight had met was now totally overgrown with briars—as the Knight so painfully knew. The Witch figured that a thick briar patch would keep the people in and the enemy out.

It hadn't been that long since the Knight had slipped suddenly into the ring and then met the boy and his sister. Only a few days had passed. Dendra's pulse rate was slightly faster than our world but not by much; the Witch had worked quickly.

She had thought for so long about what she would do once she was in charge that it didn't take her long to put her plans in motion. Even as she and the Knight had been talking, she had been thinking. The Knight was just a minor inconvenience, really. She'd been born to rule, and it was about time she got her break. She hadn't uncrossed her eyes for nothing.

As soon as the Witch sent the Knight off—to be truthful, she didn't know exactly where she'd sent him; she just hoped she'd be able to make good on her promise and bring him back in seven years—she threw some briar seeds on the ground and rode Gumples back to the castle. She sent out an announcement that the Knight had decided to undertake a dangerous quest on foot to strengthen his character and make him a better ruler, leaving her in charge. Many people greeted this news with "It's about time," or "I'm certain his character could be improved, but you'd think he would have warned us first," or "Always was irresponsible. Just like him to be so impulsive." As to the Witch being in charge, since the people didn't know she was a witch and since she didn't look much like one, they didn't seem to care. Actually, they didn't really know what the Knight looked like. Everybody looked pretty much the same in a suit of armor.

The Witch did hear a few grumbles about the twisting spell. Although the remarks made her angry, she had to pretend she would discover who was responsible and punish him. In the meantime, she planned to twist people so much that they would end up liking it. If she could only get them to think it was natural, then all kinds of things might be possible. She decided to ease up on the dying part and twist some traditions in a way that people might like.

The first thing the Witch did was to decree that everyone eat backwards. The right way, she declared, was plum pie first, brussel sprouts last—if they still had room for them. Brussel sprouts were a staple of the Dendra agro-business; cooks fixed them in every way imaginable—roasted, broiled, sautéed, steamed, batter-fried, baked. There was even a brussel sprout tart. People simply detested the things, they ate so many. It didn't take any time for people to switch their mealtime habits. The agro-bureaucrats were furious because, of course, nobody ever saved room for brussel sprouts. The excess brussel sprouts soon began moldering in the streets. The stench was becoming unbearable. Nobody liked it, but nobody wanted to go back to eating sprouts first, plum pie last.

Anyway, street clean up as a whole had suffered. Dendra had been an immaculate place to live, everybody had agreed. "We may be a lot of things," said Dendrites, "but we're not sloppy." Well, the Witch soon saw to that. She wanted to be the most beautiful object in the land, and she wasn't taking any chances. The sloppier and more slovenly the people got—other women especially—the better she would look with the least

amount of effort. Too much plum pie was helping tremen-
dously, but so was the change in the work-to-play ratio.

Work and school took only a day and a half under the
Witch's modified twisting spell. The rest of the week was free.
People could do as they pleased—fish, swim, play games,
whatever, just so long as no one did anything like work. And no
one did. In fact, no one did anything at all. A few people at first
tried to start up a bridge club, but people thought that the cards
were too heavy to hold—too much like work—so they stopped
attending. Something odd seemed to be happening to gravity.
Whether it was too much plum pie or too few brussel sprouts,
everybody felt so much heavier. Brooms and buckets as well as
bridge cards suffered the same fate. Whatever it was, the
Dendrite motto became "slow and easy." The people got so lazy
they didn't even care if others knew their real names. It was too
much trouble to guard them.

The Witch had her own minor troubles. Any spell that affected Dendra affected her as well. She didn't want to feel too
heavy to move. So, she wrapped herself in a separation spell;
even so she was bound to be affected, just as the Knight had
been when he landed in the brambles. Although his armor was
awkward, the extra weight of the spell had been the real reason
why he hadn't been able to pull himself out of the brambles.

Gumples helped the Knight right himself. He nudged and
shoved. He snorted and butted until the Knight rolled out of the
brambles and fell to his knees on the ground. Although the
Knight was grateful to Gumples, he never even thanked him for
the help. All he could think of was getting that thorn out of his
flesh. How was he going to sit in the saddle with it embedded
where it was? But no matter how many contortions he went
through, he couldn't reach it. And Gumples couldn't figure out
what the problem was. He was only a horse, after all.

After several attempts, the Knight managed to mount
Gumples and begin the slow, bumpy ride back to the castle. He
hoped he wasn't too late. "But too late for what?" he asked himself. He had no idea what the Witch might have done nor what

he was going to do once he got home. He had never been strong on planning and organization. That's why the kingdom had no second-in-command to fall back on when he wasn't around.

As he rode he looked around him. The trees and flowers looked thick and heavy—dull, too, the colors muddy, the air dense without being moist. It was getting harder and harder for him to stay in the saddle. When, around the next bend, he came upon a shady grove of trees, the temptation was too great. He pulled up, lumbered off Gumples, and lay down to rest. How long he would have lain there is hard to say—maybe forever.

Chapter 9

Beauty Is the Benchmark

Perhaps the area where our limitations are most keenly felt and where our imaginations are most needed is in our work. Some jobs, science or mathematics for example, have imagination built in. Henri Poincaré, the last great universal mathematician—some people say the last possible because the field of mathematics is too large for any one person to master—said, "A scientist worthy of the name, above all a mathematician, experiences in his work the same impression as an artist; his pleasure is as great and of the same nature."[1] In short, his pleasure is imaginative. We've seen a lot of pleased and imaginative scientists in the last few years.

This has been the century of great scientific work in all fields—from the esoteric quantum mechanics to plastics and tupperware to the double helix, computers, and everything in between—hybrid corn, the pill, antibiotics. The urge to know has compelled and controlled scientists as well as the rest of us. But along with this urge to know, science has become philosophical; scientists have naturally turned to writing. Poincaré, for example, devoted much of his time to writing popular works on mathematics; his books were read everywhere by everyone in France thirty or more years ago. To the surprise and chagrin of many novelists, he was even named to the French academy of literature.

Science magazine celebrated its fifth anniversary in 1984 by exploring twenty great discoveries of this century. Horace Freeland Judson in the introductory article says, "the sciences now do for us most of the things we traditionally demanded of the arts. The sciences surely supply profound aesthetic gratification. Scientists, and especially mathematicians and physicists, greatly prize beauty in a theory. They speak of elegance. It becomes an aspect of proof, a pointer to truth."[2] Judson quotes physicist Paul Dirac about how one recognizes beauty in an equation and where theoretical ideas come from. "Well—you feel it. Just like beauty in a picture or beauty in music. You can't describe it, it's something—and if you don't feel it, you just have to accept that you're not susceptible to it. No one can explain it to you. If someone doesn't appreciate the beauty of music, what can you do? Give 'em up!" And the theoretical? "You just have to try and imagine what—the universe—is like."[3]

How many of us have ever tried to imagine what the universe is like?

Let's try an easier question. How many of us have ever tried to imagine the universe of the business we work in?

Or, How many of us have ever tried to imagine what someone else's universe is like?

Not any easier?

How about, How many of us have ever tried to imagine what God is like?

Corrie ten Boom said we can never use our imagination too much. Most of us live as though we ought to use our imagination as little as possible. She added that even when we have stretched our imagination to its tautest, when we think we can go no farther with it, God always goes beyond it. He is always able to do more than we ask or think. Although his imagination always surpasses ours, if we have a small imagination we will yield small results. Relativity would not have been discovered had Einstein begun with a small idea. Instead, he wanted to discover the principle that held everything together, much the way Newton wanted to. Corrie ten Boom would have said that God demands that we stretch our imagination to its fullest so that he can stretch his correspondingly.

But what about those of us who aren't scientists or mathematicians? Can we find and use imagination in our work?

From What-If to Why-Not

Some people hate their work; others love it. Whichever category you fall in, and most people fall somewhere in between—some days good, some days not-so-good—imagination can help by giving you a vision of the job apart from how it seems at the moment. In any task there are the unpleasant realities—tedium, fatigue, petty details, equipment failures. Then there are the possibilities that produce satisfaction—orderliness, beauty, resolution of a problem or problems, invention, error-free performance. Those generalities fit any job, whether you are a middle manager, office worker, assemblyman, line worker, mother, or president of a corporation.

Imagination can do much to increase your job satisfaction—no matter where you fit in the spectrum. For example, although it cannot actually fix a piece of broken machinery, imagination can point to the right solution or to a way of making do until the machine can be fixed. Farmers are lost without a great deal of mechanical imagination. Sometimes bubble gum and a coat hanger are all that's available. If you can't find one part, use something that can stand in its stead. Imagination allows you to ask the what-would-happen-if questions and gives you the confidence to chance something that's never been tried before. It also helps you recognize what might work among all the whacky ideas that occur to you. Many a mother has asked herself, "Now where would I be if I were Mary's scarf?" Missing objects have been found in such unlikely places as the refrigerator, the trash can (I know of people who have thrown away their pay checks only to find them between the carrot peelings and the old coffee grounds), or the stove. Thinking of the unlikely and the unexpected can sometimes turn a frustrating situation into a successful day, as well as provide an amusing anecdote for the future.

Unfortunately for most of us, frustration happens so quickly and takes hold so thoroughly that imagination hasn't a chance. Before we know it, we're having one of those days again. Time laughs at our feeble attempts to redeem the day; once more we crawl into bed having accomplished little, having been angry a lot, and generally feeling like a hopeless failure—just like Rita.

"It never fails . . ." thought Rita. She never bothered to finish the sentence. "It never fails" said it all. Whatever went wrong was always preceded by those three words. It's a law of the universe she thought, on one of those interminable it-never-fails days; she seemed to be having more and more of them. The copy machine always broke down just when she had a rush job of hundreds of pages to deliver in a few hours. Or the typewriter ran out of ribbon in the middle of an important report. It never ran out of ribbon when you didn't need it. But, then, her computer never ran out of ribbon, she thought, just as the electricity momentarily flickered and sent her documents into oblivion. "I know that all this equipment is sitting perfectly all right in a state of total repair and elegance until I want to use it. Then, poof. It never fails."

She was thinking these and other equally frustrating thoughts the day of the party. She and her friends had planned the farewell so carefully. Rita still couldn't believe that after twelve years with the company, Joan had resigned—for no other reason than "it's time to move on." She and Carrie had invited all the departments for a soup and salad lunch, nothing complicated. The day before the lunch, Rita had reminded everyone of their various responsibilities: three people with soup, two with bread, plus salad and desert. Everything seemed under control—always the time that "it never fails."

One of the soup makers had been sick, though she assured Rita that she'd be at work the next day, soup pot in tow. It didn't quite work out that way. A recent storm had dumped a foot or more of snow on the city; country roads hadn't been plowed.

Jeanne couldn't get to a store for ingredients so she had to make do with what was in her meager refrigerator. And meager was what came out—soup for three won't feed fourteen people, no matter how parsimoniously it's ladled out. Jeanne nevertheless brought her soup to work the next day. What else could she do?

Rita couldn't believe it. But as upset as she was, she didn't want to upset Jeanne, who still didn't feel very well. Besides, it wasn't entirely Jeanne's fault. Rita asked one of the other people in the office what to do. "Salvage the soup," Jack suggested. And they did, with a few more ingredients and some liquid plus a great deal of imagination and fast work: they invented a recipe as they improvised—a new cheese soup. The party went well, after all. And the cheese soup? It was the first pot emptied, and people asked for the recipe. Rita couldn't believe that "it never fails" hadn't turned into "one of those days."

We've all had them. Days where nothing seems to go right and even the air in the office seems at war with our lungs. Every person you call is either out or in a meeting. The people you need to see are unavailable. You go to the office early to work before the phones start, but somebody sees your light and comes in to talk for half an hour. You've probably never had a soup problem at work, but the others are familiar. Flexibility in any job is a plus, whether it's in an office or in a home. Children are more unpredictable than the average office situation. Toddlers have a way of turning a clean and orderly house—all ready for Bible study or a couples' group—into the remains of a vicious bullfight. Teenagers, too, have their disruptive moments.

How does imagination help us work, no matter what the work is? It promotes and strengthens that wonderful commodity, flexibility. Unexpected situations call for unexpected responses. Our normal patterns or habits may not enable us to take potential disasters and turn them into achievements. With imagination, we can look at problems not as trials or obstacles, but as challenges to meet, goals to be achieved, or hurdles to jump as quickly as possible. Thus, Rita and her friends looked at a culinary disaster and made it the best soup at the party.

Certain people have an uncanny ability to make things work. These people use their imaginations to envision a use for their mistakes, to recognize what potential lies in failure. In fact, imaginative people probably learn more from mistakes than they do from successes.

As we have seen, science and invention is replete with examples of researchers who bungled everything, only to bungle their way to a great discovery. Luck? Probably not. It was an instinct born of a supple imagination that helped them recognize a possible success out of a failure. This has happened repeatedly in brain research. To study brain cells, scientists needed a dye that would color only one particular brain cell in a tissue sample without coloring them all. Camillo Golgi (1844-1926) discovered the dye with the help of his cleaning lady. She had thrown into a wastebasket a piece of brain tissue Golgi had been working on. The wastebasket contained some sodium nitrate solution. Golgi noticed what had happened to the brain tissue—individual cells were stained—and he had what he needed. Who knows why he looked into his wastebasket; people have strange habits (maybe he didn't want that tissue thrown away in the first place). Yet, he was able to recognize what had happened. He was a noticer. He let nothing escape him. How many of us really notice what happens around us? And then, make something out of it?

In the late nineteenth century the German dye industry had developed some new dyes for fabrics. Earlier some of these dyes had been found beneficial in treating malaria. Scientists were convinced that the dyes would probably help other medical disorders. (If it works for one, it might work for many—probably not a sound scientific principle since the chemical makeup of dyes and the chemical makeup of illnesses other than malaria could differ radically.) Through experimentation, however, doctors found that one dye in particular seemed to calm some surgical patients. It was a small step to discovering chlorpromazine, the first breakthrough in treating schizophrenia. In 1954 when it was introduced in this country, the number of patients in mental hospitals began to decline dramatically.

To the average person a leap from a fabric dye to a major breakthrough in treating schizophrenia is remarkable, strange—perhaps bizarre. Yet researchers—the good ones anyway—think no question is too strange to ask. It's difficult to overemphasize the importance of the what-if question for any of us, no matter what work we do.

The Other Right Answer

What would happen if . . . we did things a little differently, broke some ruts and habits, looked for the second—or third or fourth—right answer to a problem rather than the first. We are taught to look for *the* solution, *the* right answer, when there might be many right answers to a problem. In arithmetic, it's true there are only right or wrong answers; but in mathematics the equation is more important—at a certain level—than the answer. Remember Dirac? The equation must be beautiful. He said, "It is more important to have beauty in one's equations than to have them fit the experiment. It seems that if one is working from the point of view of getting beauty in one's equations, and if one has a really sound insight [I read imagination here], one is on a sure line of progress."[4] The same is true of the relation to theory and observation. Dirac claimed that "It's most important to have a beautiful theory. And if the observations don't support it, don't be too distressed, but wait a bit and see if some error in the observation doesn't show up."[5] Dirac is making beauty the benchmark for determining truth or rightness about work. He is unconcerned that the facts don't seem to fit the theory. If it's really beautiful, the facts will sooner or later be proven wrong and the theory right.

An appeal to beauty is an appeal to imagination. Recognizing mistakes as an answer to a previously unanswered question is how imagination transforms work from routine to adventure. Searching for and trying to create beauty is another. I doubt that many of us, whether secretaries or executives, teachers or mechanics, try to make our routines as beautiful as possible. Yet beauty, wherever it's found, has a transforming power—transforming and testing the work and transforming and proving the person. An elegant memo, for example. How many of us wouldn't appreciate one every so often? Elegant not just in appearance but in style and sentence structure, filled with funny metaphors or apt descriptions. Memos are the bane of any office. Digital voice exchange, electronic mail, and computer-transmitted messages haven't improved the beauty or the sensibility of many of them. A well-written memo can provide a refreshing pause in a humdrum day. The government has been trying for years to replace business-ese with normal language. I'd like to go even farther. A few metaphors and images, as well as clear, unadorned prose wouldn't be wasted; the writer might even get some action on his memo if he wrote for beauty.

Creating a beautiful memo is a small thing in the larger scope of a person's responsibilities. Yet, we need a place to start. To tackle the overall job might prove a formidable, overwhelming, or discouraging task. But dissecting a job—any job, whether it's cleaning a house or preparing a corporate budget—is the way to begin. Accountants, I'm certain, gain great satisfaction from columns of neat, accurate figures. They may sense that they have created something beautiful. They should be able to say it consciously.

People may be unconsciously striving for some kind of beauty in their jobs, but unless it can become conscious, it won't do them much good. People are restless and uncomfortable and don't know why; what they lack is beauty, imagination. A large statistical report, a budget defense, a paper to be presented before faculty, dictation to be transcribed, cows to be fed, fields to be plowed, or a garden to be planted all hold potential for beauty. Several years ago, a traffic cop made the nightly news across the country because of the beautiful and imaginative way he did his job. Watching him was almost like seeing a ballerina. I can think of no job less rewarding or filled with the least potential for beauty than standing in a busy intersection all day, fighting crabby drivers, exhaust fumes, and the weather. But that man thought of shape and form, of liquid arm movements and elegance—of beauty. He brought to his job a sense of wonder and imagination; he undoubtedly had asked himself what he could do to make something more out of what he had.

That is what the urge of imagination and the search for beauty in a job requires: that the person ask, What more can I make of this? Is this just a dull typing or factory job? Or is this job part of a continuum to create a beautiful, useful product? Can my small part have something of the imaginative in it? What is the challenge? I couldn't name a job that doesn't somewhere contain in it the potential for beauty and grace—either in the way it is done or in the finished product or in the initial approach to completing the job.

Unfortunately, repetitious jobs take the beauty right out of a person. Imagination falls quietly asleep. We give up, either through frustration that we cannot make our jobs more interesting (which usually means we want to get a different job rather than transform the job we have) or because we are too far behind or not busy enough. Work never seems to go just the way we'd like it to. People scramble to keep up with what they have. To think of a different way of doing a job can be discouraging or frightening. Imagination takes as much work as the work, at least at first, until imagination becomes a habit and we automatically wonder, What's the second right answer? Is there a more interesting or efficient, elegant way of doing this job?

I have had some pretty tedious jobs—grocery store cashier, for example. This was in the days before scanners and cash registers that figured the correct change. I worked in a large supermarket with twenty-three checkout lanes. We sold everything from food to clothing to small appliances. I hated that job. I stood for hours ringing up groceries for people who blamed *me* because food prices were too high and I was too slow or their kids were screaming and they forgot the checkbook or they ran out of money or . . . the list could go on. (My sister worked for the same store chain in a different location; she once was slapped by a customer.) How do you make a job like that interesting? When you've rung up one box of Tide, you've rung them all. The customers weren't interested in chitchat—they just wanted to go home.

I decided I would be efficient, fast. I also decided that I would find a couple of baggers who enjoyed bagging for me. So I learned to vary the speed with which I rang up groceries (to suit the tempo of the bagger and the mood of the customer). I developed a system of ringing up groceries where I was always ahead of my hand; that is, whatever I had my hand on to push back was not what I was ringing up. I'd taken care of that item perhaps four or five items earlier (independent of me, my sister had come up with this same system). It sometimes confused the customer, particularly if I had my hand on a quart of milk at 49 cents and was ringing up detergent at two or three dollars. Other than that, it was a great system—fast, efficient, seldom caused errors. It meant that I had to concentrate, of course, to make sure I didn't miss something. But that was the whole point. It challenged me in a completely nonchallenging job.

It wasn't quite so easy for me to find something beautiful or imaginative about typing. I don't like to type; I hated transcribing dictation tapes, though I found a certain satisfaction in the finished product—stacks of neat letters. That, finally, was what I concentrated on. Making the letters look as beautiful as I could: no erasures, good margins, clear, clean type (which meant keeping the typewriter keys clean and the ribbon new), paper smudge-free. Secretaries today would have a more difficult time to make typing letters an imaginative activity; word processing is both a bane and a blessing in that regard. It's obviously easier to make letters and other documents look beautiful, but the computer does it for you. You need to look further to involve your imagination. Beyond the appearance, though, there are other things to do. A typist can think as much as the person who originally wrote the letter. Why not correct grammatical errors, for example, or awkwardly phrased sentences? Anyone, even bosses, can misuse the English language. I always made corrections; I'm not certain the people whose letters I typed knew what I had done (or maybe they did and that's why they made me an editor, where I was supposed to do that sort of thing).

Filing was a particular challenge. As much as I wanted to make the job itself a work of imagination, I could never find a way to do it. However, the time was never wasted; a person can file quite well and do many other things, such as writing or planning a party or organizing the rest of your work schedule. Remember Einstein's job at the patent office. In his later years he was grateful he had had such a routine job for it freed his mind to fly to the problems of quanta, light particles, and relativity. Enforced, unimaginative work is not always bad. It can be a mental vacation. There are days when all of us should have nothing more to do than file; I would recommend it to managers periodically. No one really enjoys the job, but a filing day every couple of weeks would keep managers in touch with the ordinary and yet so important tasks of life (ever try to find something in badly organized files?). At the same time, they could concentrate—without realizing it—on a particularly troublesome management problem. I could almost guarantee that a solution or solutions would occur to them while filing. (Vacuuming or washing the kitchen floor might have the same result, and spouses would appreciate the help, I'm sure.) Poincaré discovered accidentally the benefit of leaving work behind. He didn't file, but he did break his routine. Traveling on a bus seemed to have triggered his imagination. Once, just as he stepped on a bus, the equation with which he had struggled for days became clear. This happened to him several times throughout his career.

Breaking Away from the Predictable

Earlier I talked about making ourselves into living metaphors. There is no better place to do that than on the job. Writing metaphors about your job—rather than a normal job description—can help you clarify how you feel about your job, and is something each of us should do periodically. It keeps us from sinking into boredom, complacency, or mediocrity. Any and every job, no matter how stimulating, can become routine. Without realizing it, a person can begin to go through the motions of work. Mind and imagination focus on nothing at all.

Limbs seem heavier every morning, as though some prankster had replaced blood and bones with cement. The thought of going to work has lost its appeal (if it ever had any). Assess yourself, your job, and your co-workers through metaphors. What images come to mind when you think of how you are performing your job? What metaphors do you think of when you think of the job itself? A person may be unaware that he thinks his job a prison or a maze with no way out or a mousetrap and he's the mouse, tail securely caught. He may not know that he feels as if he's working for Bluebeard or Attila the Hun or that he is Atlas with the weight of the world on his shoulders. Maybe he feels like a train conductor who can never run his train on time and has thoughts of throwing himself in front of the train wheels. Of course, there may be pleasant surprises, too. A person may find how much he enjoys his job.

Bringing imagination to a job does not require a supervisor's approval. I suspect that many people are waiting for someone above them to say, "Go ahead. Be imaginative." Many people want someone else to give them ideas on how to be imaginative in a job. Perhaps they want a new job that they think will be more imaginative and challenging than the one they have. Unfortunately, most supervisors won't do any of those things. They're too busy worrying about their own jobs to give much thought to the people under them (this is true even though the job of management is to find and keep happy, stimulated, and challenged employees). The responsibility lies with the person himself. It is no doubt true that many jobs must be done from top to bottom or left to right. But maybe some things could be done bottom to top or right to left or even sideways. Do you need to sit at a desk to do your job? Could you do it just as well standing up at a chest-high shelf? Or sitting on the floor? Maybe the job should be rightside up and you be upside down (Mary Poppins would approve of that).

Do you have a report to prepare? Why should it be written in business-ese? Why not use a little imagination in putting it together? Write an article. Or a feature story on the subject of your report. Write it as a mystery, giving the reader clues along the way as to what the outcome of the report is going to be. Don't produce the same old charts or graphs. Use cartoons instead. It might take a little effort to move your imagination, but once you get used to thinking this way, it will become effortless. Your imagination will not be the resource of last resort, but the first faculty that starts in motion even before you walk in the front door. You will enjoy your job a lot more; if you aren't enjoying your work, no one else will, either.

Teachers as well as people in business can find themselves in the same rut. How many times have they taught the same material to the same types of unresponsive or surly students who only want the hour to end? The teacher may have used the same book and the same lectures and the same basic tests for years. The subject may bore him; it does the students, too. Why do students gravitate to a certain teacher? He may not be any more knowledgeable about the subject, but he may be more imaginative in how he teaches it. There will always be students who don't want anything unusual because an unusual approach will force them to use their minds and imaginations (there are people who, no matter what you do, refuse to use imagination, much to their detriment).

I know a minister who feels that he is forced into predictable, rigid patterns because of the busyness of his life. He knows that he should read outside his field—that is, books and magazines that seem to have no logical or readily apparent connection with preaching, counseling, or running a church, yet he rarely does so. The few times when he has done so have made him a better preacher and counselor; he has more ideas than when he sticks to his business. Because imagination doesn't necessarily work along predictable lines, ideas can come from anywhere. If more professionals read widely outside of their field—or became involved in activities totally unrelated to their profession—they would become better at their jobs, would have the unusual idea now and again, and would begin to solve problems more quickly. It's a hard habit to break, this compulsion to keep up in the field (some of that is necessary in any profession). Perhaps the goal should be to balance the amount of time spent keeping up in comparison to the amount of time spent learning something new.

Much of what I've been saying can be summed up in one word: beginning. Gladys Taber in *Stillmeadow Calendar* says, "I decided the secret of happy living is to keep a few beginnings on hand. The happy people I know are always beginning something—it doesn't matter much what it is."[6] Any job has the potential of beginnings, as does play or relationships. In a sense, each day is a new beginning though I think what Taber has in mind goes beyond that. Always have a few new projects or ideas on hand—small or large. Beginnings keep a person's imagination sharply honed: first you have to think about them; then you have to do them. Thomas Edison probably had more beginnings on hand at any period in his life than was reasonably good for him. Yet look at the contribution his imagination made. People who always have a few beginnings on hand are never bored. They make certain their imagination has something to work with. Boredom can be a great motivator in stirring the imagination. Not that people who begin things are driven by boredom; I doubt that they are. Rather, they are driven by the desire to experiment, learn, discover. But for people who haven't lived that way, boredom can be a motivator to give it a try. Restlessness and dissatisfaction on a job often comes from the person himself, not because the job is boring or unchallenging. Students who learn little in school, those who merely go through the motions, will never be happy or satisfied. Nor will an employee.

No Matter What the Job

You might protest that Taber's observation is fine for people whose professions are inherently stimulating. Or that it's fine for hobbies (we'll get to hobbies later); but it wouldn't work in your job. You have to do the same things in the same way every day. There's no room for you to begin something on your own. Edward de Bono, a consultant to the corporate world on imagination, once replaced a $90 lung machine with a 25 cents whistle. A lot of people thought his idea was crazy; but he proved that it would work. Although there are people who feel threatened by fresh ideas and new approaches to a job, most people—once they get used to the exhilarating air of imagination—relish beginnings. There is always a better, faster, more interesting way of doing a job than someone has thought of before. Start with your own job and see what transformations you can work there. Some jobs have more strictures, it's true, but rather than view that as a drawback, let it be an even stronger incentive for imagination.

The person with the most potential for imagination on the job is the person who cares for the home, be it man or woman. A homemaker to a great degree can set her own schedule, if not at the beginning and end of a day, certainly throughout the day. There is opportunity to experiment with meals, organization, cleaning, and childcare. If no other job will do it, caring for children will keep a person's imagination hopping. Children don't have the adult strictures on how to see reality. They haven't reached the why-bother stage, when no one cares to ask questions because we know there are no answers (or at least we think we know). People who work at home and care for children can begin something new every day of their lives. No one will tell them not to rearrange their office furniture. No one says that coffee break occurs at 9:45 A.M. and 2:45 P.M. and only then. There is no reason why cleaning and the laundry and cooking need follow a pattern, unless the person is most comfortable with that.

Naturally, even here you have other people to consider: children, spouse, perhaps other relatives who live with you. It is possible to train others to accept some experimentation, particularly in cooking. All of us are born with neutral tastebuds, rather like we're born with the ability to make many sounds our particular language may not use. Taste is a learned response. What people like depends to a great extent on what they're used to. That's why mommy's cooking is always better than a friend's mommy's cooking. Once you get your family to broaden their palates you will have freed their imagination to allow you to turn the daily drudgery of planning and preparing meals into a feast of color, smell, texture, and taste. There's no reason to be stuck with brown, dried up meatloaf with a blob of dark red ketchup on the top. Mashed potatoes are not a pre-requisite to a good, balanced meal, no matter how many people insist upon it. Vegetables need not be mushy, colorless, taste-less affairs. Nor does soup have to come out of a Campbell's can. There was chicken noodle long before the red cans ap-peared on supermarket shelves. Cooking is one of the most imaginative jobs a homemaker has. The endless varieties of chicken recipes alone could keep someone experimenting for years. Nutrition-conscious cooks can discover low-fat, low-salt, and low-sugar menus, all delicious. Vegetarian meals need not consist of soy meat substitutes. Why look for a meat substi-tute at all when vegetables are so good? *Homemade* and *from scratch* are not dirty words.

The packaged food companies like General Mills and others have managed to convince the American public that life is not possible without convenience foods. There are some canned goods worth buying—canned tomatoes, for example, or tomato paste (if you can find the no-salt-added variety and you can't can your own). But soups and mixes are not worth the sup-posed convenience, any more than frozen breakfasts or dinners are. You live a fast-paced life, shout the advertisers; so they offer us bread that's more like cotton candy and frozen pizzas like cardboard. Busy people don't need to settle for anything less than the real thing. We have taken from homemakers one of the greatest challenges to imagination. Most of them don't realize that they can make their own bread without sacrificing inordinate amounts of time; that they can cook meals from scratch that are better for their families and easier on their food budgets; that a birthday cake comes from somewhere other than a Duncan Hines mix. Once a homemaker and family smell bak-ing bread and taste the rich, chewy texture, they will never re-turn to store-bought again. No bakery can make bread as good as a person can make at home, either. You will pay four times as much to buy a comparable loaf—as comparable as possible, that is. With the new faster-rising yeasts recently introduced on the market, a person can make a couple loaves of bread in two hours or less. Realize, too, that as the bread is rising, the bread baker can do something else—read, clean, iron, feed the baby, shop. Breadbaking makes little demands for the great satisfaction the end product gives. Homemakers are dissatisfied because imagination has been stripped from their work.

Boredom and its partner restlessness can become hard companions to leave behind. A person can use the imagination God gave him, or he can become so enmeshed in their company that imagination has no place to sit down. Everyone, whether employed full-time outside the home or within it, has household responsibilities that can either drain a person's energy or contribute to it. Those stuck with energy-draining attitudes and approaches to household chores would benefit from imagination.

People compartmentalize life. Work at home is one kind of thing; work at an office is another; childcare or gardening yet another. Work and play are separated, as well. With all those compartments, it takes time and energy to move from one area to another. That is wasted time. Life should be seen as a whole, lived as a continuum. If a person isn't using imagination in his household responsibilities, what makes him think an outside job will prove any more stimulating? Ultimately, how challenged a person is, or how restful or restless, depends on the person, not on circumstances. If imagination is left out, changing jobs or houses will not solve the problem. The impetus compelling someone to work should be the same whether it is mowing the lawn, balancing the budget, or feeding the family. The fulfillment a person finds in his play, his leisure, should be no greater or different than that he finds in his work. Work and play are part of the same whole.

Chapter 9, Notes

1. E. T. Bell, *Men of Mathematics* (Simon & Schuster, 1937), p.526.

2. Horace Freeland Judson, Introduction, *Science 84* 5, (November, 1984): 42.

3. Ibid., p. 43.

4. *Science 84*, pp. 42,43.

5. Ibid., p. 43.

6. Gladys Taber, *Stillmeadow Calendar* (Lippencott, 1967), p. 47.

Chapter 10

Just Loving

People think of work and play as different, the one necessary but unpleasant, the other pleasurable—the reason to live. Yet with imagination work is a pleasure; without imagination play is no fun.

During childhood, playtime is worktime, the way children gain maturity. They learn to share, to compromise, to imitate their parents or the other adults they know. Play has meaning; it isn't random, nor something to keep a child quiet and occupied, a way to fill or kill time. Today's toys for young and middle grade school children, however, are too sophisticated; they require little imagination. Children forget—if they ever learn—how to play make-believe or let's pretend. They become dependent on gadgets to entertain themselves. The television is not the only offender. Toys are battery operated, remote controlled, microchipped. What once were common toys are now hard to find—so hard in fact that last Christmas a Chicago merchant offered traditional toys in a fancy "sidewalk box," a colorful plastic carrying case that held a jump rope, a set of jacks, chalk for hopscotch, and a few other simple playthings. Individually, the toys would probably cost a few of dollars; the sidewalk box sold for more than ten dollars. Thus, old-fashioned becomes fashionable with some smart packaging.

What does a child have left to imagine? Tinker toys and erector sets are much fancier than they once were. Now whatever a child builds must work—move, spin, climb. A child doesn't make a car go, providing the "vroom, vroom" himself. He pushes a button at a distance from the car, and it runs. Plain, honest blocks are fast disappearing. Even five-and six-year-olds want computers or computerized games.

Paralleling this decrease in toys that stimulate imaginative activity is a shrinking of children's attention spans and abilities to concentrate. Watching much television dramatically decreases a child's ability to visualize stories or ideas for himself; it reduces how long he can focus on any given topic. Little children naturally have short attention spans. Part of their maturation is the ability to concentrate for longer and longer periods. Yet high-tech toys reinforce a certain restlessness and inability to focus on anything for more than a few minutes. For example, children have difficulty reading for any significant amount of time. Black ink on white paper doesn't have the visual appeal of a color television or the computer graphics in Donkey Kong. There's no denying that. But of course the black ink on white paper is not meant to be looked at in quite the same way as a video screen; children only know how to look in one way.

Words on a page, words that show and say and do and invite and stir, take a little work to understand. Every word attached to every other word attached to sentence after paragraph after page after chapter after book should open worlds upon worlds for the reader. Each word should be more potent than the best Saturday morning cartoon or the funniest situation comedy. But the words themselves don't move, dance, shimmy, gyrate, talk, bounce, or do any of the things that words do on Sesame Street. They just sit quietly on the page, waiting for the reader's mind to do all those things. The words point to meanings the reader must supply, to understanding and imagination and movement and color and excitement that takes place not in front of a reader's eyes but behind them. If all entertainment happens to a child outside himself, soon there's nothing inside with which to respond.

People need what my mother called "inner resources" in order to overcome circumstances, whether they be a not-so-interesting and challenging job, a boring teacher, or the more serious and potentially damaging events of life. People need inner resources to entertain themselves, too. Playfulness is an attitude, a way of seeing and approaching life. Today many children play with no sense of playfulness; the same is true for many adults. It's very difficult to break habits formed in childhood. If a person is always entertained, he will never learn to entertain himself.

Children, and adults too, I suppose, have a difficult time making the transition from being entertained to entertaining themselves. The first summer in Michigan was such a transition for our nine-and eleven-year-olds. The boys assumed that they could watch television all day. When they and my husband lived on the east coast, they had been in a highly structured summer day camp where adults supervised all their activities. Suddenly they were in the country. Television was off-limits—and just plain off day and night; they had to read an hour a day—a mean requirement their father and I decided on, and they had to make up games or suffer the consequences of boredom. For a while, they chose boredom. Day after day I would return from work to find them sitting outside, doing nothing—which is what their father said they had been doing all day—nothing (apart from certain chores and reading, that is). They were obviously unhappy, obviously bored, but they didn't know what to do about it. How do you tell children how to play, how to entertain themselves? As a family, we began reading aloud the most imaginative books we could find. My husband and I suggested the obvious games—cowboys and Indians, cops and robbers, climbing trees, exploring the shallow creek behind the house, hiking, bikeriding. They had been used to a narrowly proscribed territory, roughly equivalent to a ten-minute ride from the house. Although they no longer had such boundaries, they still adhered to them, rather like animals who still think the electric fence is in place long after it has been turned off, or a prisoner who becomes used to restricted living quarters and finds it difficult to deal with more space. In effect, the children were prisoners of a society that ignores or devalues what we can't see or touch and yet nevertheless has a great impact on us, a culture that ignores or cheapens the work of imagination (Saturday morning cartoons, for example). Rats in a maze will respond the same way; they will not realize that the walls have disappeared and that they can travel where they want to.

Many children and adults live within nonexistent walls. Whether society makes us think they exist—or our parents or we do—is unimportant. These walls can become so thick and high that we never ask if they can be surmounted or leveled. Yet they can be. Every person's walls are different; ask yourself what yours are. Your life, both play and work, could become incredibly rich.

Getting Back to Eden

At the beginning of this chapter I said that people distinguish between work and play. Work is what someone makes us do when we are young—go to school, do chores—and what we do as an adult to feed and clothe ourselves. Many people work simply to have money to enjoy themselves when they aren't working. Work is rarely viewed as pleasurable; the very definition of the word argues against it, as does the curse in Genesis. Most of us spend as much time and money trying to find our way back to the garden where the fruit was easy to find and the body and mind were unencumbered. People choose different routes to travel back there; they even have different gardens they're looking for, but it all amounts to the same thing, escape. Some people drink, others eat or ski or hunt or fish or play tennis or sleep or watch television or yes, even read. People take up hobbies for the same reason. There are as many different ways of getting back to Eden as there are people.

Yet the assumption that work began when Adam and Eve were expelled from the garden is a peculiar one. The original couple had chores to do, as anyone who has ever had a garden knows. They may not have had weeds or blight or pests or verticillium wilt. The racoons may never have eaten their Silver Queen corn at the very peak of ripeness. But someone had to harvest the fruit, and if not they, who else? Trees and shrubs surely needed to be pruned. Animals needed to be named. I'm certain there were many details to care for in running Eden; it was probably just easier without weather problems or soilborne diseases. But it isn't that they didn't have to work.

The curse said that from then on when Adam and Eve worked they would sweat, groan, and ache. Gardening without weary muscles or soaked skin is almost beyond imagination. Yet that was the state before they left Eden. Afterward, as they scratched their seed into the ground and pulled out weeds by hand, they undoubtedly looked back on Eden and said, "And we thought *that* was work." There's always something harder in a person's life, something that requires greater effort than he has previously made. It's all a matter of perspective. What one person thinks of as work—gardening, for example—another person might find a joy, not work at all. The person who loves gardening might admit that it is hard, but just because something is hard does not make it work. Work and play should be— and in some instances people think of them as—the same. Both the work for which we are paid, and the work that we voluntarily choose to do as a hobby or as recreation can be joy-filled.

Lots of people busy with vocation and several avocations suffer from dis-ease, in spite of, or perhaps because of, their busyness. It's difficult to keep a sense of joy and wonder when at the point of exhaustion. We all know people at both ends of the spectrum—those who have lost their sense of wonder through living lives of quiet misery; unhappy at work, unhappy at home, unhappy at church; lives who are being fed no imaginative meat or spiritual nectar. Everything about them seems gray. We know people who seem perpetually active with work, hobbies, social engagements, community and church commitments, and yet seem to gain no satisfaction from how they live.

Their lives, too, are dreary. Simple pleasures don't exist, whether it is pleasure in prayer and worship, pleasure in a job well done, or pleasure in rest.

Perhaps that is the problem: no rest, no silence, no time to think or love or stretch the imagination. Everyone needs such times. God told Adam and Eve to keep the day of rest holy; he understood that people need time to stare into space, time to daydream or sleep or wander wherever imagination takes them. Gladys Taber tells of a little boy who intuitively understood the potential rest can hold for us. He sat for hours one day on his grandmother's porch, cat beside him, teddy bear in his lap. Finally his grandmother had to ask what he was doing. "I'm loving, Grandma. Jus' loving."[1] Not many of us, I suspect, spend any time just loving. Those few words from that small child give me his character, his attitude, his complete delight and joy in life. He didn't need to be doing anything to know it; he only had to stop and watch and feel it surround him. Adults who know the exultation in being alive may be able to express themselves more descriptively, but no one could express it more completely than that child did. The life within him reached out to touch the life around him. He became, not a little boy with a cat and a teddy bear watching the trees and sky and flowers, but life itself, life incarnate. Those mystical moments may not come often in a lifetime, but when they do, a person never forgets them. They were C. S. Lewis's times of joy, that little boy's time of loving.

The ultimate incarnation of life and imagination was, as we have seen, Jesus. Perhaps because he knew he had to die (we all know that, of course) and die in such a horrible fashion (that none of us knows), he retained his sense of wonder. He lived on the edge of expectation. He reached out to meet what came to him, whether good or ill: He was ready. Most of us never expect anything, so there's nothing to reach out for. Even the ordinary things, the daily routine, give us no sense of expectation; predictability, yes, but not expectation. Yet Jesus loved it all—the ordinary and the extraordinary. He knew that the ordinary was as exciting and important as the extraordinary. The little boy wasn't loving the unusual; he was loving the usual—what surrounded him every day. If we can't keep a sense of wonder and awe about the everyday matters of life, we will have no wonder ready for the special times.

Imagination presents us with the possibilities of wonder. It can bathe our eyes and limbs with cool cloths of light so that we can walk awake through the business of living, whether it be work or play. Playtime or recreation or avocation, whatever we want to call it, is not a matter of finding a few hobbies—some other work that we choose to do apart from our vocation. Imaginative off-hours are as much dependent on what we don't do. Reading or woodworking or fishing or needlework all can enlarge imagination and increase a sense of wonder. Any activity where we make something will bring us closer to God. His nature takes shape and definition through what he makes; we more closely reflect his personality when we make things. But we aren't God, and even he needed a day when he didn't make anything, a day when he collected himself and his thoughts. Because there's so much to do, we don't want to do nothing— though a day dedicated to thinking could hardly be empty. But other people watching us sit in front of a fire or lie peacefully in a hammock could very easily assume that we're having a lazy day. Without such times, though, we won't have the imaginative strength and excitement to help us enjoy our avocations.

Expanding Our Palates

It is also possible to spend too much time in preparation, as Ann did.

She was educated, she said to herself. Well, presumably educated. She had an advanced degree to prove it, if only to herself. She had a stimulating job. Yet her restlessness, or perhaps weariness was a more accurate word, had to come from somewhere. No, even weariness is wrong, she thought to herself. She was spending lots of time trying to determine what it was that she felt. She loved life and her life, it was true, but she also felt empty. Not the spiritual emptiness that her friends talked about, not the kind of thing the minister preached about on Sunday. That was defining spiritual too narrowly for her anyway. It wasn't conversion that she needed; nor was it dedication or re-dedication, despite the numerous altar calls she heard week after week. But she definitely felt a lack in her soul, a nourishment she was missing. As a person with scurvy craves oranges, she craved . . . orange, or maybe color. Or sounds. Or words. Or textures. Everything seemed so drab; she needed some bleach to brighten things up.

She followed the same pattern every week. Work for five days, getting to work early each morning. At night she read and went to sleep. From Friday night until Sunday morning she rarely saw or talked with anyone. She stayed in her apartment reading. She read novels and mysteries mostly, sometimes five or six books in a weekend. She loved reading; she loved good storytellers. She enjoyed habit and pattern. She knew she wasn't bored. She had more intellectual stimulation than most of the people she knew. But her interests were so narrow—a certain kind of music, a certain kind of book, certain colors (green mostly, because it reminded her of the outdoors), certain outdoor activities (sitting by the pool in summer; she wasn't one for working up a sweat).

I live in a narrowly proscribed world, she thought . . . predictable . . . only those challenges I can handle and limited to a few areas. My life is much the same no matter what the season. I'm out of rhythm with nature, which may mean I'm out of rhythm with God. The animals are closer to him than I, following the instincts he has put into them from summer through winter and back to summer, from night to day and back again to night. Air conditioning and heating fuel, supermarkets and truck farms have made every season pretty much the same. About the only thing that changes is the length of daylight, arbitrarily lengthened by Congress. The closest she came to any rhythmic approach to life was to put away her winter clothes and wash and iron her summer ones. For animals, she thought, it's a whole lot easier. They just grow thicker coats in winter and then shed them when it warms up.

She thought back to her childhood. Her life had more trueness about it then. The seasons were clearly demarcated; her mother didn't allow her to hibernate permanently behind a book—certainly she didn't lack for intellectual stimulation, or did she? Her father's garden seemed to grow so effortlessly—huge pumpkins, beans, peas, potatoes, tomatoes in abundance for summer fresh eating and winter canning. How did he grow all those things so easily? She didn't remember him ever working at it, certainly not weeding. It was almost as if his garden didn't have the audacity to grow weeds. She vaguely remembered the seed catalogs in winter, Burpees especially—who could forget a name like that?—and she knew that he started tomatoes from seeds, but beyond that, nothing. Oh, except for the compost heap, which was nothing fancier than a pile of leaves and grass clippings, she supposed. What she really remembered was the harvesting. That was woman's work—or in her case, girl's work. She especially hated picking beans. The feel of bean leaves and bugs left her skin crawling and itching for hours afterward. She hated bugs with a passion. She didn't mind snipping bushels of beans or shelling peas. A person could do that indoors watching a baseball game or soap operas. But outside in the hot sun . . .

Yet it nevertheless provided a definite beat to life. Fresh produce in the summer, grown a few feet from the house, not covered with chemicals and cellophane from the store. In winter, canned produce that tasted much fresher than canned goods in the store. Looking back on it, she knew she had wasted a great opportunity to learn something important when she had ignored her father's garden or her mother's canning efforts, her mother who made the best bread and butter pickles in the world. She was also puzzled why, beyond picking and snipping, she didn't have to help her mother in the kitchen. Teachers made sure you learned history and arithmetic and grammar, she thought. But there was a lot of other stuff she could have learned if she had only wanted to or someone had insisted that she learn.

Those memories triggered in her a desire—not to have a garden, that came later. They triggered a desire to broaden her interests. Just because she wasn't bored, that didn't mean she didn't lack something. She began experimenting with food, with needlework, with ideas and books. She tried to look beyond what she knew and was comfortable with to learn something she didn't know, maybe didn't care about, but that might interest her if she tried. She was surprised to find that she became interested in so many things, liked so many colors, enjoyed so many tastes and textures. She had never liked fresh fruit, apples in particular, so she went to the store and started eating apples; she soon loved them. She did the same with bananas, pears, grapefruit, plums, mangoes, papayas, kiwi, and every other fruit she could find. She had always loved most vegetables, but she tried vegetables that she would never eat as a child: tomatoes, scallions, turnips, parsnips, spinach. She wasn't sure why she decided to start with food for her life-expanding exercise, but food was so fundamental and so fraught with symbolism for the Christian that it seemed the only place to begin. From eating foods she didn't like, she moved to making food by hand that she did like; bread, primarily. Kneading bread gave her deep satisfaction and a chance to think clear thoughts while her hands were in thick dough. One day while working at some bread, she realized that she had allowed her imagination to slow to a crawl. It was barely moving, suffocating for lack of oxygen and energy. She had been feeding her imagination the same food every day, not that the food wasn't good—it just didn't contain all the nutrients her imagination needed; the ideas she encountered were all the same.

Slowly, she began to expand her reading tastes beyond fiction into nonfiction: history first, then philosophy, psychology, and science. The essay form was making a resurgence in the publishing world, so she read essayists both serious and humorous. She investigated art forms that she had hitherto ignored, such as painting and dance. Although musically she was well-educated, particularly with the classical literature, she began to listen to modern composers and moved away from the eighteenth century. And then country music, a form she had always disliked, suddenly had its appeal. For the first time, in more than an intellectual way, she realized God had provided such abundant variety that it was wrong to have restricted herself. It was as though coming to a banquet of rich tastes and glorious smells, she had chosen water and a crust of bread because she'd eaten them before. Was she timid, fearful, distrustful?

The desire to make things strengthened; baking bread eventually didn't satisfy the urge. So, prodded by a friend, she began to make afghans, rugs, sweaters, pillows, pictures, chair covers. She started growing plants indoors, and when she had the opportunity, began to grow flowers outside and eventually a vegetable garden. In high school she had detested outdoor work. Now she discovered how much she enjoyed putting her hands in warm dirt with a rich, earthy smell. Something about it cleansed and stretched her mind like nothing else ever had. It seemed as though she couldn't get enough life growing, blooming, dying back, and growing again. Reading other books and magazines soon followed, books about the emotional appeal of the wilderness or the fascinating scientific facts about nature.

The more she read and made during her off-hours, the more productive and excited about her job she became. The lines between work and play disappeared. But the ideas she received during her recreational time stimulated her imagination nine to five, Monday through Friday. She was able to see problems as challenges, see the whole where only pieces existed, and put into proper perspective problem people or situations. Her imagination worked constantly. She no longer had to strain for ideas; they surrounded her as did oxygen, carbon dioxide, and hydrogen. She realized how many years she had wasted. It was particularly clear to her when she began reading science journals and thought back to her high school science days with her dread and dislike of anything other than English or history. She laughed at her old self, so far removed from who she was now.

Caught in Compartments

One woman's journey from dull, unimaginative, and stultifying existence into imaginative living; she could be any one of us. The commonly held belief in our society that as we grow older our mental faculties—mind and imagination—slow down, that only in youth do we possess sharp wits, is false. People retire earlier and earlier, though the life expectancy of the average person continues to increase. But because those same people may never have exercised their mind's eye during off hours, they don't know what to do now. They use up their interests quickly; their imaginations have almost completely atrophied, blocking the possibility for new ideas to enter. Yet as I said earlier, stimulation can make a difference.

Kay Marshall Strom in *Chosen Families*, a book on adoption, tells of a couple who adopted a six-month-old baby. The child had few of the responses she should have had at that age; she couldn't sit up, roll over, or hold her head up, for example. The couple took Lisa to a doctor, who gave them the bad news that Lisa was retarded. They couldn't believe it, wouldn't believe it. "We planned our strategy. Gary took a month's vacation and we spent hours and hours playing with Lisa, holding her, stimulating her in any way possible. The results were amazing! In three weeks she had caught up to where a six month old should be. She was alert, active, sitting well, even starting to crawl. The doctor was astounded at her progress."[2] When a mother says a baby is alert and active, she is also saying that the baby is curious, evidence of normal imaginative activity. This couple's experience shows what can happen to a normal six-month-old who, through neglect or abuse, has become stunted. Although stimulating the imagination won't make a handicapped child non-handicapped, it will nevertheless increase the abilities the child has, as teachers and parents who live with such children will agree. What is true for infants and young children may also be true for older people. We can continue to expand our minds past the age when society calls us old.

Barbara Pym has written *Quartet in Autumn*, a terrifying novel of what happens to four people in retirement. It is all the more terrifying because it is so ordinary: a simple style to tell the tale of four fellow office workers. One of the four loses all perspective and slides slowly into deshabille and death, for no other reason than that her imagination has ceased to function.

Without the strictures of a nine-to-five existence, the woman has no reason to eat, dress, bathe, live. It is no doubt an extreme story; yet it is also a metaphor for many of our lives. We stop growing shortly after we finish school; nothing remains but the grave.

In compartmentalizing our lives into work and play, we have created areas for the sacred and the secular, despite all the lip service we give on Sunday that we live as Christians throughout the week. Not that we are insincere; we just have no idea what it means to live as Christians at all times. We think it means to avoid sin, which is part of it, certainly. But Christianity is not just living without, it is also living for. It is the positive, not the negative. A wise pastoral counselor once told me that if Christians concentrated more on worship and less on avoiding sin, they would soon have fewer problems with sin and a more abundant relationship with their Creator. What you stare at is what will consume you; if you stare at sin, even to avoid it, sin will be uppermost in your mind. We need to fill our minds with God; he cannot live in a dead environment, though he can transform one. Living on the edge of expectation, as Christ did, is part of our stewardship as Christians. For example, most of us, because we separate the sacred and the secular, interpret the parable of the talents to mean that we are to multiply our spiritual activities, give more money and time to the church, and so forth. We don't think that it also might mean expanding our interests, stretching our imaginative muscles, growing in our understanding of the life God has given us. This needn't mean great amounts of money spent or time for travel. It can be simple, ordinary things that provide the understanding. Any life-producing activity is a spiritual one. Any stretch of the imagination can have repercussions beyond yourself. Barbara Webster in *Creatures and Contentments* said, "Who knows how many times the everyday-ness of a woman digging in her flower-bed, or two children riding a fat pony, has served to save someone from despair?"[3] She is right.

When you begin to live with imagination, you develop new patterns of behavior, whether at work or play. But the kind of growth and expansion that true stewardship requires cannot be achieved without time alone. Everyone needs it. Time to think, to pray, to dream, to stare into space, to allow the imagination free reign. Christ knew and practiced that principle. Without his times alone he might not have been able to withstand the temptations he faced; nor would he have handled the intense pressures of his job, the people pressing on him with constant demands. We cannot get a vision beyond ourselves if we don't stop moving. Imaginative living is to achieve a balance between the business of life, the learning and challenge of new ideas, and the quietude of isolation. The balance point is different for each person. Some people need more contact with other people; some need more time alone, just as some people need more physical exercise than others. Still others need more time with ideas to stretch themselves. They live, as Einstein and others did, in at least two worlds simultaneously. And the most important one may be that which occurs in their imagination and mind.

For some people and some professions there is no distinction between work and play, not because they see work as play and play as work, but because all life is caught up in one thing. In a sense they have neither worktime nor playtime, but merely time, all of it dedicated to their vocation. They are a special group of people for whom the normal principles of imaginative living cannot apply. A pure mathematician, a rare person, is such a one. Nothing exists—not day or night or eating, sleeping, relationships, or even self—to a pure mathematician: only the abstract mathematical idea. A scientist, for example a physicist for whom mathematics is essential to his work as a tool, cannot understand the pure mathematician, for whom the idea is important in and of itself. New mathematics at the time they are invented have no practical purpose. (Thus, no Nobel Prize is awarded in mathematics.) They are just ideas; the only relationship a mathematician has is his relationship to his own imagination where the ideas develop. Eventually a scientist will need the mathematics, as scientists needed the calculus. Most of us might think of someone sitting alone with paper and pencil and ideas as the worst sort of work. The mathematician is unaware he is working; he is unaware of his surroundings, of himself, of his physical requirements. Mathematics, and perhaps musical composition, may be the purest example we have of imagination at work. Because of its strenuous demands, many mathematicians suffer severe anxiety or breakdowns. The history of music, too, is filled with the lives of tragic composers. Although the life of a mathematician is not an example for most of us—a person is either born with mathematical talent or he is not, and most mathematicians reach the end of their imaginative powers early in life, as a swimmer reaches the end of his physical prowess early—the singlemindedness is instructive. Most of us suffer not from too much singlemindedness, but from not enough. We are easily seduced from our goals. It takes discipline to be a Christian with an imagination awake and ready to receive God's grace. It requires effort to take the talents God has given us and multiply them. It takes judgement to know where the balance lies, how much time to spend cultivating the various areas of life to bring them into balance. Whether working or playing, to use imagination properly and to the fullest we must alternate times of imaginative exercise with times of imaginative rest.

Make Mine Homemade

The principles of imaginative living apply equally to all areas of life, and if we do apply them equally, life will no longer be a series of compartments—work, recreation, service, relationships (which binds all other areas together), and times alone—but will be whole. I cannot stress enough that what we do in one area will affect and to some extent determine what we do in other areas. The metaphors that we use at work will influence the metaphors we choose when we aren't working.

Work is such a necessity that in many respects it's easier to deal with. We have Jesus as a model of how to perform the work God has given each of us to do. He singlemindedly performed his work. Yet, it didn't interfere with his relationships, perhaps because his disciples and other followers were so intrinsic to his work. People are not an intrinsic part of many people's work; certainly not for a pure mathematician or for a factory worker or the local UPS driver, though they are in some way affected by people. But, did Jesus play? Did he have any off-hours?

If by play we mean those unimportant and less significant times in life, then, no, Jesus had no time off. He was always on the job, the first to put in a lot of overtime (for which we should all be grateful). Yet, if we look at life as a whole, ignoring the artificial distinction between work and play, ignoring that work is supposed to be drudgery and play is supposed to be enjoyable, then Jesus had a full social calendar. He had numerous dinner engagements, for one thing, times when he was the grateful guest to a gracious host. Many of his invitations came from the wealthy and the powerful. He no doubt rested on the Sabbath. We know he played with children when his disciples thought he had better things to do. Yet at times there is nothing better to do than play with children. He also guarded his times alone when he could pray, meditate, or dream without the press of the crowd. He escaped in a boat. Nothing is more peaceful than to sit in the middle of a lake.

So Jesus, too, followed the principle of rest or isolation. We know he thought of himself in metaphors. He dined with friends and acquaintances (and enemies, too). He stretched his imagination by frequent contacts with people quite different from himself—sick people, fearful people, children, people with whom he disagreed. He used what was available to him to stretch his imagination. He never shirked a challenge; nor did he ever deliberately argue about issues, but sought to get to the heart of what the questioner was asking. Jesus undoubtedly knew the importance of using imagination to make things. He learned the carpenter's trade from his father. The touch of wood is a glorious sensation. Paul followed in his footsteps by being a tentmaker (though in his circumstance it was probably more to feed his body than his imagination).

We can challenge ourselves today in a different fashion— not just by talking, but by reading and studying. We aren't dependent on a craft to earn our living, so we can practice many crafts throughout our life. It is easier to get away from everything and everyone. (But only in some senses. There are few places left today without crowds of people, mammoth hotels, and tasteless souvenir shops. I'm not sure Jesus would be able to find a quiet place in Israel today, even in the desert. He and Satan would have had to find someplace else for their momentous confrontation.) We have a great deal more time to spend doing things other than feeding, clothing, and providing shelter for ourselves. We can grow our own food for fun, not out of necessity. We can bake bread from scratch, but only because we want to and not because there is no other way to have bread. We can hook our own rugs, make our own quilts and afghans, sew our own clothes, even weave our own cloth if we want to. It isn't even necessary to buy furniture; there are still people today who make their own.

We've turned these once-essential crafts into hobbies. What we once did because there was no other way to own certain things we now do for pleasure. Here again the line between work and play shifts and swerves. Making a quilt was not only to create something beautiful; more important than its beauty was its ability to keep people from freezing in unheated bedrooms; it also showed frugality as well as imagination to take scraps and make something new and useful. What once was work has now become play. There may be things that we now consider work that future generations will view quite differently. But who was having more fun—the women who made quilts out of necessity, but in a quilting bee, a social situation, or a person today who by herself may make only a few in her life? We do many of our hobbies alone, cut off from conversation and our neighbors.

A hobby by its definition is something nonessential, perhaps frivolous—collecting stamps, for example, or milk glass. Yet many people do not approach their hobbies frivolously, nor are the results frivolous. Hobbies are something a person can do without, something to pass the time—as if time needed any help in passing—something to keep a person

occupied so that boredom doesn't stalk him. People facing retirement are told to take up one or two. But doing something
just for the sake of being busy isn't the answer for an empty life.
Such activity is meaningless. The results will look it; the person
will feel it. To get captured by something, to give one's
imagination to it wholeheartedly, can be a great pleasure. One
imaginative activity in a person's life will inevitably lead to
another and then to another. People who live with imagination
rarely function that way on one or two levels; their lives are permeated by it. Because they live with Roman candles constantly
exploding, such people are infectious to be around. They help
others catch a vision for a different type of life, one where we
can be participants and not spectators, one where we can put
something back, rather than deplete, one where work hours and
recreation time are part of the same continuum and equally
pleasurable. Life for such people has an innate rhythm and balance. They instinctively know when to separate themselves
from the crowd, as Christ did, and when to have a party. People
who live imaginatively also have a strong sense of the nature of
time as something to reclaim, a part of the stewardship we have
at our disposal, just like money or talent. Time is not something
to cram full of antiboredom devices. Rather it is something to
serve; it has a life of its own. An imaginative life is a life in balance and proper perspective. This is particularly true when it
comes to relationships.

Chapter 10, Notes

1. Gladys Taber, *Stillmeadow Calendar* (Lippencott, 1967), p. 56.

2. Kay Marshall Strom, *Chosen Families* (Zondervan, 1985), p. 54.

3. Barbara Webster, *Creatures and Contentments* (Norton, 1965), p. 231.

Chapter 11

A Witching Principle

E ven after so short a time, the Witch was getting tired of ruling the kingdom. Really, she thought to herself, there's not that much to do—especially now. Something's missing. Some challenge. Some spark I thought sure would be there when I took over.

Not only was the Witch tired of doing nothing—she'd fulfilled her plan in a few days and the people had put up so little resistance—she was tired of protecting herself from her spells. That expended more energy than avoiding the Knight all those years. Her plans had been pretty simple. Just a few hours ago as she moped about the castle, a timid little courtier had tentatively suggested that she take up a hobby.

"A hobby!" she had cackled. (She nearly had given herself away with that one, she knew. She could almost feel a wart and half a hair start growing on her nose.) Hobbies were for bored wives of agro-bureaucrats. She could certainly see why they needed them. Fixing brussel sprouts day in and day out would drive anyone to the primitive arts. But she had all the marsh-grass wall hangings she would ever need here in the castle, no doubt presents from grateful subjects. Imagine. A hobby for someone of her stature and importance, for one of her gifts and

145

abilities—such as they are, she thought dismally. Some days she wasn't as confident as she might have been. If she'd had a teacher, she might have gone far. No use moaning about what never was, she told herself more and more often in the last few days.

She was wise enough to know she needed more spice in her life, but unwise enough not to realize that without the Knight around she had no match in the kingdom. In a land where no one knows your name—where you aren't always certain you remember it—it's comforting that someone at least knows who you are. That's what the Witch missed. Dendrites would never be impertinent enough to ask, "Who are you?"

Dendrites are dull sparks, at best. The timid courtier was acting quite out of character in making any suggestion at all. If the Witch had known anything about trout fishing, she might have found something to challenge her there. Even keeping weeds and bugs and wildlife out of Dendra's many gardens would have kept her busy, challenged, and frustrated for years. (She knew absolutely *no* spells to get rid of slugs and potato weevil or prevent powdery mildew.)

A thought was teasing the Witch somewhere in her left or right hemisphere. Or maybe it was on the tip of her tongue. Anyway, it was there somewhere. She almost didn't want it out in the open since she'd made a big point of saying "seven years." She had figured it would take her that long at least to need a little diversion from ruling. But a few days? Where had the Knight gone? Could she get him back now or did she really have to wait the full seven years before he returned? She wasn't too certain what the spell codes called for at this point. Would it be violating a witching principle to return him so soon? She didn't know, but she decided with some exasperation and asperity that it was worth considering. Since she did her best considering while on a horse, she decided to go for a ride. If she stayed around much longer, she thought she might tear down the castle walls or eat her way through the kitchen. Her clothes had been a little snug when she dressed that morning.

The Knight had settled—it almost seemed permanently to Gumples—under the tree. No amount of nudging or bumping affected the Knight. Not even the throbbing thorn made him want to move. It's amazing, thought the Knight, how one can get used to anything. He did not realize that he had stumbled on one of the Witch's favorite haunts. Just then she rode up.

"So you're back," said the Witch. "How'd you get here? Seven days aren't even up, much less seven years." (The Witch sounded pretty brusque, but actually she was relieved. It solved the greatest ethical dilemma of her life.)

"Some girl sent me back," replied the Knight slowly. "But that's not important. What have you done to Dendra now that you're in charge? You don't seem any different, but everything seems slightly cattywhampus."

"Witches never change. Anyway, I've got a separation spell wrapped around me so I'm not affected by Dendrite air and weight. You see, I made everything heavier. Just as an experiment.

"What do you mean, heavier?"

"My, you are dull. Anyway, that's only one of the things I've done. Everybody's got a lot more free time now. Not that your Dendrites are putting their free time to good use. They just sit and stare vacantly around them. The lawns and flowerbeds are in a mess. Actually, the town is getting to be pretty unattractive. It's hard to see the flowers for the weeds. I don't know. I may move."

The Witch startled herself when she said this—confiding in the Knight. The Knight for his part was equally amazed. Not that she had confided in him, but that she could be so unreasonable. If the town was out of hand, who caused it? Dendra might not have been the best and the brightest, but it had a certain charm.

The Knight thought he saw a way to get his kingdom back without a big brouhaha. That wasn't really his style, anyway—despite the fact that he wore his armor everywhere he went. And in this air—suddenly he noticed his throbbing flesh again—he was in no mood or shape for fighting. But a little gentle persuasion? The Knight summoned all the oratorical skills he had. He slowly drew himself up to his full height and cleared his throat stentoriously. He needed now, if ever, to make an impression.

"Lady Witch," he began. (Not bad, he thought to himself. Keep going.) "We have long been enemies. You have teased and tried me sorely in the past" (not to mention this thorn, he thought). "You have twisted my land and my efforts to keep people busy, happy, and whole. You have wanted to rule; I have resisted your efforts. Further, . . ."

"You're taking too long to get to the point," interrupted the Witch. "Tell me something I don't know, like where you went when I sent you off. I could do it again, you know. Right now."

With those words, she raised her arms and voice dramatically. "But I won't. Too much trouble. Too dull without you."

"May I continue?" the Knight asked in his best regal tones. And really his voice was quite regal when he wanted it to be. The Witch was almost impressed.

"Only if you stop being so stuffy and get to the point. OK, so you don't like my simple, clever, cute, and wondrously troublesome twisting spells. Right. Got it. Knew it long ago. But what else was I supposed to do? You were born a knight, I, a witch. Just following destiny, so to speak."

"You have a point, of course, which I was just getting to." He dropped his regal manner. "I can see how you wouldn't be able to stop being a witch, but do you have to cause trouble just because you are? I mean, that's the whole point, isn't it? You are a witch and not a ruler. I'm a ruler and not anything else. I'm just trying to do my job, but you keep trying to do mine. Why, I think your twisting spell worked on you first, before it hit any of the Dendrites."

"Well . . ."

"Let me finish. I'll admit you're probably a little cleverer than I am. I don't have anyone in the castle with quite your gifts and abilities. You must know some grand spells, as well as those little mean ones. With a little more study—we've got quite a library, in case you don't know it—you might become better than you are. Even I know that some of your spells must be junior league. We might make a good team. You could help me figure things out and I could help you appreciate and enjoy Dendra a little more—after we get it cleaned up, of course." He had just caught a whiff of something very unpleasant.

Chapter 12

Cleaning Out the Corners

S omeone has said that a failed relationship is a problem of a failed imagination. No matter what the relationship, imagination is the crucial ingredient for success or failure. Marriage relationships either thrive or die because of imagination, as do relationships between parent and child, co-workers, employee and employer. Imagination helps a person persevere and stay committed. Imagination enables a person to envision the possibilities in the relationship—or the consequences of ending it. It helps a person work in isolation from everyone else; it supports recreation. But the true test of imagination comes in how it helps you relate to—understand—other people.

Jesus used his imagination in his work—yet unlike our other models, his vocation could not be separated from his relationships. People were his vocation. When Jesus said love your neighbor as yourself or treat others as you want to be treated, he was stating a fundamental principle of imagination. Self-centeredness can have no part in imaginative living. An imaginative person is too aware of the other fellow to be totally wrapped up in his own wants or perceptions. I know how I want to be treated; therefore I know how I should treat others.

Respect, courtesy, thoughtfulness, anticipation, and a sense of joy and discovery in the relationship are all necessary ingredients to a mature, close friendship.

The story in the gospels about Jesus and Zaccheus is a case in point. Of all the people in the crowd that day, Zaccheus was probably the most unloved, certainly the most isolated person. He, a Jew, had joined the Romans and was collecting taxes from Jews—money the Romans used to keep the Jews in subjection. He was also shorter than everyone else. In a country where people are naturally short and where because of diet people were much shorter than they are today, Zaccheus must have been quite small. He probably despised himself for his size, his job, his lack of friends; he was wealthy, yes, but undoubtedly unhappy. Otherwise why go to such extremes to see Jesus? Whether you call it Jesus' empathic powers or his imagination (to me empathy is a result of a fervent imagination), Jesus recognized a need in Zaccheus. First it was for human contact. So he invited himself to Zaccheus's house for dinner. Although Jesus seemed to violate every principle of hospitality, somehow he got away with it. Jesus didn't immediately start preaching to Zaccheus that he had to change his way of life, rid himself of his undoubtedly hard-earned money, give to the poor, walk in justice, and so forth. Zac needed to do all those things, Jesus knew. But first he needed a friend. He needed the opportunity to provide hospitality to someone. He needed to give at a level he could understand before he could understand giving in other ways. Jesus made himself available, thus leading Zac to see what he should do. Jesus left that meal having brought about a transformed life.

Unfortunately in most of our relationships we skip over the first step and move right into the second or third. We fail to treat people with respect and dignity, even though that's how we want to be treated. We are busy classifying people, almost unconsciously, as worthy, not worthy, constantly isolating those who don't seem human to us (or those we don't intend to treat as human) from those who have in our eyes attained human stature. Every day we define someone as nonhuman. Zac was a nonhuman to the Jews. The Jews had lots of nonhumans, let's face it. They had problems with Jesus because he insisted on treating everybody as human, as creatures of God: thieves, prostitutes, rich men, poor women. He also claimed to be God, which was another sticky point with the Jews; of course this was the claim that explained his revolutionary treatment of people. We're not immune to that problem today. Everything in us wants to categorize and group people; we thrive on cliques, inside knowledge, exclusivity. Jesus' imaginative life cuts through that like a scimitar.

Jesus always took time to learn about people. Some he understood instinctively; others he watched for a longer period of time. Many of the people he loved were undoubtedly unlovely; yet he knew he could at some point be unlovely too.

He asked himself—and us—what-if questions. What if that were I? What if I were so unfortunate? What if I had lived through what this person had lived through? His command to love our neighbors as ourselves is based on just such a question. What if you were your neighbor? he asks. What if you were the man who had been beaten and robbed? How much would you care about ritual purity? How much would it matter to you that a Samaritan helped you and not a Jew? These questions came from Jesus' ability to create powerful, stirring images. He didn't let people rest. He prodded their imaginations into thinking about the answers; even today we have no choice but to think about those questions.

If there is any area where imagination is weakest, it is in relationships. We can be imaginative at work or at play when we are primarily dealing with ourselves. But in a relationship we must think of the other person first; otherwise no relationship is possible. We should base a relationship on our desire to give to and serve the other person. It is no doubt true that many relationships are one-sided. Although the other person, too, should try to do the same, it doesn't always happen that way. A parent-child relationship, for example, will always be one-sided until the child is mature enough to respond in kind. An imaginative parent will always be on the lookout for things to stimulate, broaden, expand, or challenge his child's interests. He helps a child discover what he is good at, where his abilities and talents lie. And then he points him in the right directions to develop those talents and abilities. But a child is not conscious of this happening. Probably a good parent would not want his efforts to seem out of the ordinary, unnatural. Any parent expecting gratitude or appreciation for his behavior will be disappointed. Although parents should teach children those virtues, only later, when a child remembers and recognizes what he received from his parents and is able to put it into context, may he respond gratefully. We can accept those conditions with children; with adults it is more difficult.

Reserved for Discovery

Unfortunately ingratitude exists in too many marriages. A failed marriage is without question a failure of imagination— each person unable or unwilling to become the other person imaginatively. He or she didn't enjoy, respect, or concern himself enough to discover the other person's what-ifs. "In most of the unhappy marriages I know about," writes Gladys Taber, "neither of the partners seems to be interested in making discoveries about each other. . . . [Yet] the world itself brings discoveries almost daily."[1]

Imaginative living involves making discoveries, whether it's about work or play or your friends, neighbors, family, the world you live in, or God. That's why Jesus was so exciting to those who met him. He lived on the edge of expectation, anticipating each day, each new discovery. Most of us, though, don't see excitement or wonder in anything we do or in anyone we know. What daily discovery does a wife make about a husband or a husband about a wife? Maybe that happens at first, but after a few years when routines and habits are set? Yet how much happier would a marriage be if the couple determined to discover something new about each other every day and at the same time to forget something unpleasant. Most people, it seems, insist on discovering as many unpleasant things about each other and forgetting any interesting or unusual traits.

Because bad habits are hard to break, perhaps couples should start with a more modest goal: instead of every day start with every week. To make room for all the new information, some old stuff must go. Lewis Thomas thinks that one of the most marvelous characteristics about the brain is that it allows us to forget some things to make room for others. Although much of our forgetting is beyond our control (as when we've just forgotten the name of someone we're about to introduce), we could help our brains by simply refusing to remember certain things: irritating habits, unintentional hurts or spites, miscommunication, words said in anger. Then, if we insist on discovering something new, and concentrate on those things, our brains will eventually clean out a corner for them. Envision a space up there under your hair—or where your hair used to be—and mark it "reserved" for all the discoveries you will make in the next weeks and months and years of your married life. You'll be able to throw away every marriage manual you ever bought. This principle of discovery will work for every relationship you have, whether good or bad. The good ones will get better, the bad ones will improve dramatically: So will your interest in life.

This principle also works with the spiritual life. Most evangelicals became Christians early in life. We're raised in Christian homes; we've read the Bible many times over. Jesus is no stranger—we think. Long ago we decided we had learned all there was to know about God and his Son: presumptuous, no doubt, as though a human being can ever reach the end of God. Yet we live as though it were true. We're not in the business of making discoveries about God. Rather, if he wants us to know something, it's his responsibility to tell us as obviously as possible. When we do "study" God, it's always in a particular setting with a particular set of props. But a person need not be in church or Sunday school or a Bible study to get friendly with God. Fortunately for us, God's grace operates everywhere—otherwise how would we earn a living if we had to spend all our time in Bible study and prayer? For some reason, we never expect to learn anything new about God. But if we can discover new things about people we've known for years, why not with

God? (In the next chapter, we'll talk about how to make discoveries about God.)

People are endlessly fascinating—ordinary people as much as extraordinary or famous people, sometimes more. Those of us who spend a lot of time and money reading biographies (or *People* magazine) should spend an equal amount of time and money studying the people around us. How many times have we been surprised, almost amazed, by the things we know about ourselves, but other people don't? Ann Landers has kept her column alive with letters from husbands or wives who write that they've been married twenty-five years and just discovered that _____. It might be nice to think that after twenty-five years, couples are still making discoveries about each other, but the tone of the letters usually suggests that it's the first discovery they've made in all that time. Parents can fall into the same trap by assuming they know their children well. How many mothers have been astounded by the things their adult child likes? Or, how many parents still insist that John doesn't like pumpkin or that Susan has always disdained vegetables, when the reverse is actually true? Parents—and most of us—take no account of change and growth. The shrub never blooms; it forever remains a cutting.

People change and shift, excited at one time in their lives about reading mystery stories and years later scientific essays. We can never be fully known, thus it is unfortunate that so many marriages do die through lack of imagination. None of us can excuse ourselves by claiming that for years our spouse hasn't done anything interesting to discover. We just haven't been looking or listening. Listening is a primary way of learning what others are interested in and then remembering what they've said. Aren't we pleased when a host or hostess remembers how we like our coffee—or that we don't like coffee at all—or that our favorite dessert is bananas foster? Such small matters make for good hospitality, as well as good friendship. Hearing and remembering the odd detail indicates more about your feelings for a person than expensive presents or fancy words. There is a corollary to the discovery principle: if someone tries to discover things about a spouse or a friend, it could challenge him to expand his imagination, if only to give him something to find out. Imaginative living is contagious.

Three Cheers for Mental Clutter

Lewis Thomas has called the brain an old-fashioned attic, where we store all sorts of once-useful stuff, memories we're attached to, junk that we can't throw away no matter what. Modern psychiatry wants to clean up the brain—remove the clutter—much as modern architecture has deleted the attic. Yet people need clutter for imagination. We never know when something we've stored up there is going to drop down and mean something again. For our relationships, too, the stuff we store can become important. Although there is much to be said for honesty and openness, there is also much to be said for not revealing everything. First of all we probably don't know what everything is. Our spouse could discover something we left up there years ago and now could use more than anything. My husband grew up gardening, building steps, and landscaping; his parents loved plants, yet he decided he detested it and never planted so much as a handful of grass seed. When I pleaded with him—before we were married—to help me plant rose bushes, he grudgingly agreed. Since then we've moved to the country, planted flower beds and trees everywhere on our three-and-three-quarter acres, as well as a large vegetable garden. He has built a rock garden, a patio, steps into the side of a bank, a sixty foot retaining wall, and started on another rock garden. He loves it, but wouldn't have discovered it unless I needed his help with those rose bushes years ago. What if he'd removed all that unused information?

In *The Magician's Nephew*, C. S. Lewis uses the clutter of a cabby's memory to bring Frank back to himself. Now a London man, Frank was once a country boy who sang in the choir and served at the altar. Newly created Narnia awakens in him the memories of grass and trees, the smell of dew and clover; he longs to stay, which, of course, is just what Aslan has in mind. In that instant Frank is transformed. But what if he had rid himself of his country clutter? Would he have become the first king of Narnia? We may be missing some exciting possibilities, too, if we insist on sweeping away the cobwebs so thoroughly. We may also deny someone the pleasure of giving something back to us, as did Aslan with Frank. We don't want to live with nothing to be discovered—or recovered.

Of course, we can't deliberately withhold information about ourselves so that our spouses will have something to discover years later. But we can live as though there is something wonderful and mysterious about ourselves—and there is. Thinking of ourselves that way will also help us think of others in the same way.

Life is a wonder—magical. We need more of newly awakened Narnia's excitement and awe about what we are and where we live. We take so many things for granted, such as the simple ability to speak. Remember the animals' excitement as the chosen ones in Narnia began to grow and talk? The intricacies of nature are vast and miraculous. But how many of us care enough about God's work to read about it? Human personality, of course, is his crowning achievement. Yet we treat each other as lower than the most humble pet; some husbands and wives lavish more attention on a dog or cat than on each other. A human relationship is one of the most magical aspects of our lives.

That we can know, care for, and laugh with another human being should be sheer joy. Gladys Taber made it a practice to sit for a certain period each day and think about the wonders of living. What amazes you? Your list may be different than Taber's, but just as thrilling: hair, fingernails, muscles, colors, fur, gleaming wood, stone and stonework, the ocean, a fighting fish on the line, the planes and curves of your spouse's face. Make a list of amazements—and thank God for them. Or, make a list of things that should amaze you and don't, and ask God to awaken your imagination. Keep a people list—friends and acquaintances—and a spouse list. Keep an animal list, a vegetable list, a mineral list. Read a book that you have absolutely no interest in—*The Mathematical Experience*, for instance, or *The Hunt for Red October*—and *get* interested. We all might do well to imitate Taber. In our anxiety to study spiritual matters, we have forgotten that just appreciating the mystery is sometimes study enough. And worship enough. Our relationships may not have such external excitements as travel or wealth, yet the internal excitement of companionship and comfort can be more satisfying.

"Life is not, for most of us, a pageant of splendor but is made up of many small things, rather like an old-fashioned piecework quilt."[2] As anyone who has made a patchwork quilt knows, it takes years to gather the scraps and leftovers, then painstakingly and patiently piece the scraps together into a beautiful, imaginative pattern. A finished patchwork quilt is not only beautiful but also useful—warm, comforting, inviting—a good image for what our relationships should be and how imagination functions. Each of us is made up of scraps that didn't quite fit the garment at the time. We leave the leftovers everywhere—in the attic, the closet, under the bed, tucked away on a shelf. It often takes another person to discover them, puzzled as to why such beautiful fabric was left to molder. The whole can become much more than the sum of its parts when we stitch with imagination. Mismatched colors, ragged edges like disparate pieces of several jigsaw puzzles, patterns that make no sense at first sight, can all blend together when pieced as a quilt. Our patchwork lives may take years to finish, but that is part of the wonder and joy of living.

A quilt cannot make itself; nor can we. Contrary to what modern psychiatry tells us, becoming ourselves is something we needn't worry about. Our business is not to discover ourselves, but God and others. It is other people's business to discover us. We need spouse, friends, and acquaintances whose imaginations show us what we can become; God working through them to make of us a one-of-a-kind patchwork quilt. We're in good hands. And, of course, our hands will be too busy piecing together a quilt for someone else to interfere with the stitchers working on ours.

Chapter 12, Notes

1. Gladys Taber, *Stillmeadow Calendar* (Lippencott, 1967), p. 254.
2. Ibid., p. 38.

Chapter 13

Only Today

Twentieth-century psychiatry has developed along two major lines: Freud, who looked at the individual in isolation, and William James, who saw the individual in community. Our era has been marked by a search for identity—the self alone trying to discover who, what, and why he is. Until recently, Freud has been preeminent. But as people realize that *who* and *what* a person is can only be known in context—whether it be a family, a church, a business, a social community—that is changing. John Donne was right: no man is an island. It's taken us a long time to regain our perspective.

Finding imagination is both an individual and a corporate venture. It may begin with a person, but unless it leads him to someone else, his imagination has failed. A person should not want to live an imaginative life simply to gratify his interests or to stave off boredom, though if it takes boredom to get started, then be grateful for boredom. Imagination is the *imago Dei* in us; how could we keep that to ourselves and truly reflect our Creator? A vehicle for grace, imagination at times may be the only means of grace for God to use to reach some of us. Imagination, then, to be valid and active must lead us away from ourselves and to other people. But it has another and perhaps most important function: it should lead us to God; it should lead us to a reverent heart and a bowed soul; it should lead us to worship.

With all our striving for self-knowledge, we've forgotten that our primary purpose is worship. Some of the most unhappy people I've known have been those obsessed with themselves. They have been most conscious of supposed hurts and wrongs done to them and most unconscious of the hurts they inflict on other people in their slapdash wielding of themselves. A person consumed with himself not only has no time for other people, he has no time for God. Yet the act of worship, paradoxically, brings us to ourselves; the pieces fall in place. Our relationship to a large and often frightening universe becomes clear. We stand no better or worse than our fellow worshipers. God is all. We're back to that uncomfortable statement of Christ's: he who loses his life for my sake will find it. Loss of self is not something any twentieth-century person, Christian or not, finds easy to accept. Freud's philosophy has permeated our air and water too greatly; William James may never be able to compete.

We not only have trouble accepting a loss of self—perhaps imagining something like Nirvana, where our spirit joins all the other spirits in one undifferentiated mass—we haven't the vaguest notion of what worship is. (Before leaving this paradox of losing and finding ourself, let me add that God has promised us a resurrection. Somehow we will lose ourselves; but at the same time we will not be lost—the individual whose unique characteristics and quirks were lovingly bestowed by God. We may lose sight of ourselves, all well and good. But God won't. Again, all well and good. He will see us as we've never been able to see ourselves no matter how much we've gazed. As we gaze at God—which is part of worship—we may find, surprisingly, that for the first time we can see ourselves correctly as a reflection—which is how it should have been all along.)

A Life of Worship

Worship is something that happens on Sunday morning, more or less successfully, depending on the ability of the choir and the minister to stir some watery emotional response in us. Worship is not something we do; it is something that we watch happen. Even in liturgical churches where congregations must kneel—a good practice, as it symbolizes what should be happening in our souls—as the form of the service moves from confession to praise to petition and back again to praise, it is difficult to adore our unseen God. If we have trouble worshiping in a formal setting, what do we do during the week? At work? On vacation? Worship is not a punctuation mark—"praise God"—after every sentence, nor is it one line petitions to God to help you find your sweater, or book, or missing report, or whatever else crosses your mind that you need. (Not that I think these things are wrong and should be avoided; I don't; but a person who does them may not really be worshiping God.) Worship is an attitude of the heart and a function of imagination. Whatever else might happen as we strengthen our imagination, at least one thing should result: worship, the summation of life.

Worship is not, necessarily, deep, overpowering emotion. Worship is not, necessarily, singing hymns of praise. Or prayers of thanksgiving. It can be all of those things, or none. Worship is also all those things we've been talking about—right work, right play, right relationships, making ourselves living images to God. To put it into theological terms, worship is stewardship, service, sacrifice, commitment, reverence, humility, losing your life in Christ. For a life to be a life of worship, these things must happen daily, hourly, minute by minute, not just weekly.

Although formal worship is important, informal worship is at least as important. Most of us attend church on Sunday to worship God (whether the worship is true worship is not my point here). But that's as far as we go. We don't understand the kind of worship that should never cease. Work can be worship, as can recreational activities or deep relationships. Not only can they be, but they ought to be. People joke when they claim that they can worship God just as well on the golf course or at the lake, using it as an excuse to ignore corporate worship. What they don't understand is that, though it isn't a substitute for the other, worship at those times and places is just as mandatory as participating in a formal service.

Imagination can help us maintain an attitude of worship. Imagine that God is the one to whom we report on the job. Hold in our imaginations that God is the author and finisher of all good things as we garden or fish or swim or skate or read—or do whatever we do for relaxation. We need to cultivate an attitude of immediate awareness of what life means so that we see the spiritual aspects of what we do while we do them. It's a matter of learning to live on several levels simultaneously. Jesus certainly did this. We're very much at home in this world; after all, God created us especially for it. At the same time we are restive and uncomfortable here. Life is not as it should be; we see death everywhere, a constant reminder that something is wrong. If we don't learn to live in at least *two* worlds simultaneously, we will never understand life at all. Perhaps that is why it seemed easy for Christ to live on the edge of expectation. He was always prepared for the spiritual to break through into the material world. The two worlds exist together, whether we can see both or not. Do we expect the spiritual world to break into our ordinary, pattern-filled material world? Would we recognize it if it did?

We expect the spiritual to appear flourishing trumpets or performing miracles. It usually comes to us just as Jesus did, in human form; the kingdom has come. God has placed on his earth the elements of his spiritual nature, but we're not really interested. Developing an attitude of worship is to be awed by the majesty of God and his works. We are awed by very little. Science and psychology, so we think, have dispensed with mystery and pretty much explained everything to most people's satisfaction—or if they haven't done so completely, they soon will; it's just a matter of time. Not so. The more we learn about ourselves and our world, the more we don't know. In a way, it's true, we understand more than we did in Newton's day, but in other ways we know far less. How can what seems to be true be true—matter and antimatter, quarks and quanta, objects that appear to be in two places simultaneously, mitochondria that live a nearly independent life within each cell in our body, perhaps descendants of some ancient bacteria, and yet essential for life itself (it turns protein into energy, which the cell needs to function), the astounding facts being uncovered by current brain research. The list could go on indefinitely. We have an amazing, intricate, incredibly imaginative God to have invented us and our world. We have an amazingly unselfish God, as well. How many of us would have imparted to our creatures so much of our own essence, our imagination? We see the results in music, painting, dance, poetry, fiction and nonfiction, in the craft arts as well as the fine arts. But how many of us have bothered to look closely at what God has done?

We ignore God's work with the excuse that we are spending our time getting to know him directly through prayer, Bible study, and so forth. These should not be ignored. But what about all the rest? We could no more know a chef by ignoring his food than we can know God by ignoring his creation. We need an insatiable curiosity to know, and we don't have it. Knowledge feeds the imagination, which will translate into worship. It can't help but do so.

Seeing God's Face through His Works

What can we learn about God merely by looking at our world? Not a deep study, just a good use of our eyes. God is enormously inventive. He took a few basic shapes, one and two-dimensional figures, and made the most of them—triangles, squares, rectangles, straight lines, parabolas, circles. A straight line alone might have been enough, since there's an almost limitless amount you can do with it. Combining certain of these figures gives us a cone or a cylinder, three dimensions from one or two. Every object we see has one or a combination of these basic shapes. Painters learn early to see the geometry of life; modern painters rather than abstracting objects merely paint them in their fundamental state without all the dressing God has given them (we could accurately call the cubists the fundamentalists). Then God added light and color, which is another kind of light. There are just a few basic colors from which the almost limitless array of tints and shades come. But don't dismiss light because it provides the shadows, the variations within a color, the depth of certain objects that might otherwise appear flat and uninteresting. Without light, shapes and colors would be meaningless. For those of us with a less imaginative or well-trained eye, God has provided people who have captured light on canvas, Turner and Monet, for example; the shimmer and gleam evoke a poignancy that cannot be satisfied until we see Light itself. But such painters point us in the right direction.

God is not only the God of shape and light and color, but the God of texture as well. Our hands and eyes cannot have enough texture—rough, smooth, slippery, crinkled, soft, nubbly. We are fortunate that our language contains so many adjectives about texture. Every object has its own—a birch is different from an oak, which is different from a rose or peony or straw flower. In the hand and in the mouth, snap peas feel different from snap beans. Beets, turnips, carrots, and kohlrabi, though they share the same earth as they grow, have different skins, different textures when cooked or raw. Aren't we fortunate that not only our hands and our eyes, but our tongues and mouths also sense texture? (Ask anybody who is revolted by lumpy potatoes but adores the silk of whipped cream.) Corn has several textures in one plant—rough, silky, crunchy.

As if those four weren't enough, God also added scent to his creation. The earth itself, warmed by the sun, has a rich musky odor. The plants, vegetation, trees, and shrubs it nourishes—as it nourishes us, as well—also have their own particular scent, some more discernible than others. Horticulturists in their zeal for hybridization have all but destroyed the scent of certain species. Who wants a lilac bush that doesn't smell like lilacs? Or peonies or marigolds (I'm one who happens to like the pungent scent of marigolds; don't breed their odor out for me, please). There's nothing better on a warm summer day than to walk past my front border and catch a whiff of the sweet alyssum I plant around the edge every year. In the winter, when color and scent are largely absent, the odor of thorn apple burning in the fireplace is a marvelous refresher.

What we can see and touch and smell, though, almost pales beside what we can hear. The sounds of God are miracles in themselves. We could reduce that even further and talk about the sounds of birds or the sounds of a particular species of bird or the bird just outside our window. Or we can talk of bird songs or bird calls and cries—the loon, the goose, the duck. Birds are fascinating creatures. Neurophysiologists have been studying them for some time to discover how they learn to sing. Their music is more intricate than the most florid *bel canto* passage in a Bellini or Donizetti opera. Each pattern has meaning, apparently, and many species must learn the songs anew every year. Some young birds are not born knowing the notes; they're only born with the potential for song. Every spring, whether or not we are aware of it, we hear nature tuning up, birds practicing their pitches, working to get rhythm and intonation and coloratura passages just right. A mistake could mean no mate that season. Birds learn more than one song—several, each as intricate as the other. Their songs mark them, differentiate them from other birds of their kind and of other kinds.

If birds have the solo performances, we have squirrels and chipmunks who play the continuo, woodpeckers who sit on drums, frogs on tuba and double bassoon, crickets working the violin, ducks and geese on trumpet, crows on trombone—all playing together harmoniously but without a visible conductor keeping them in time. We have the privilege of a free concert day after day, but fortunately their performance doesn't depend on our appreciation. They play whether or not we listen. Is it possible to appreciate Beethoven or Mozart or Mahler unless or until we have satiated ourselves on nature's music? These concerts are acts of worship by God's creatures, not that they have volition as we do, but they are worshiping their creator by doing what he intended them to do. That's an achievement we find hard to sustain for a few hours, much less days, weeks, months, and years.

And yet in some ways it should be easier for us than for the animals to worship God by being what he intended us to be. We have memory; birds don't. We don't have to relearn our songs of praise or songs of duty each year. We can recall what we've learned and use it. We can recall past care and comfort and rest in that. We can remember the notes we've learned and sing those. Without memory, individual and collective, would we be able to worship at all?

We know that God's world is wonderful. That is, we know it intellectually, but perhaps not on an imaginative level. It's wonderfulness is outside ourselves; it never touches us. But we can't learn to worship without ceasing unless God's work in every area of life touches us imaginatively. Most of us waste the years we spend in school; we're too young to understand the importance of discovery. School should be reserved for the mature who know why we should learn—to love God, not love him better or worship him more, but to become love toward him: to embody it, incarnate it. Fortunately, we don't need a formal classroom (anymore than we need a formal sanctuary to worship in) to discover what we ignored in school. We have an active publishing industry that produces entertaining, informative books by beautiful writers who love language as well as their subject. Forget about dry textbooks. God doesn't teach us that way; his lessons are vivid, imaginative, striking—stretching every nerve and sinew in us. Of all people, Christians ought to be the most in awe of God's work; yet many of us are the most ignorant. A person cannot be amazed at an achievement unless he understands something about it. We know very little about God's achievements. Worship God by feeding on knowledge.

Curiosity about God is not just curiosity about how he deals with us—why certain things happen or don't happen to each of us. That is often the extent of our interest in God; we're interested only as far as it personally, directly affects us. Anything else about God is inconsequential. The reverse should be true. We should have the least concern about ourselves, and the most concern about all those other things. We need to forget about ourselves and learn about the birds or the lilies of the field. We should praise him for his works. Cataloging the wonders of God is a good exercise; it keeps *us* out of our imaginations, and God's work firmly implanted there. It is comforting to realize the intricacy of the universe and the imagination it took to fit all the pieces together. The detail is incredible; no computer could handle it. Yet the universe more or less functions as it should. The hands in charge are competent ones. We need to know and remember this.

God is not an impenetrable mystery; yet his ways are past finding out. We have mislaid that part of the paradox. Yes, God can be known; he has revealed himself to us in his works and in his words. Yet he can never be known completely while we're on earth. He is beyond us. We cannot see his face, but only his shadow, only his back parts. But even those back parts should be sufficient to cause us to worship. If the planes and angles, the colors and prisms, the wet and the dry, the rough and the smooth are only his back parts, what must his face be like?

Imagination will awaken our eyes to see as clearly as we can those back parts of God. We must train ourselves, work with our eyes and imagination, force them open if necessary. If we have difficulty spying the shadow of God, what will we do with his face? Read books whose authors have more acute eyes than we. Then leave the book and look around with those eyes. We have much to learn about God's work—nature, our own bodies, the microcosmos as well as the macrocosmos. We need more of the childlike curiosity that drove Einstein and Newton. We need more of a sense of playfulness and wonder about life. We're so busy trying to learn spiritual lessons and discern God's will that we have no time for God himself. Pure appreciation, wondrous delight, God as the great discovery—these are the attitudes imagination can foster in us. Just as husbands and wives stop making discoveries about one another, so we stop thinking of God as the greatest adventure of all, the most challenging discovery there is. More marriages could do with the sheer enjoyment of one another found in the Song of Solomon. But so could more God-man relationships. The Song of Solomon is stuffed full of wonderful metaphors and images that excite the imagination and tell the reader of the unabashed pleasure the lovers find in each other. God in creating the world and calling it good certainly expressed his delight in what he saw. A playful glee, a child's "There. Look at that," is the attitude in Genesis 1. Perhaps there's also a sense of wonder on God's part that even he could create something so marvelous as the world. Not boastful. Not proud. Just wonder-filled. A new mother and father after the birth of a child probably come closest to that attitude. God delights in us, his creation. But do we delight in him, our Creator? Or are we too busy trying to find out why he hasn't done this or that or what certain events or situations mean? We find it difficult to thank him for the obvious—bones, thumbs, big toes, teeth, heart, liver, pancreas, much less those things we can't see or feel and probably have only heard of briefly in a high school or college biology class, things like DNA, mitochondria, the corpus callosum, or bacteria. We don't like Latin words. We can't pronounce them. Why should we know anything about them? Because the more we know about what God has done, the better we will appreciate him.

Christians have always appreciated God's marvelous act of salvation. The Crucifixion and Resurrection are the linchpins of our faith. We have concentrated on those and ignored any physical works, implying by our behavior that only his spiritual works are important. Yet the Incarnation as well as the Resurrection contradicts that attitude. We are physical creatures, put into a physical world, whom God loved enough to plan and execute the Incarnation. He gave Jesus back his body— better than the original, no doubt—when he brought him back to life. Jesus lived in a world of sand and scrub trees and seas. He loved the feel of wood and water; death was no easier for him than it is for any of us and for many of the same reasons. We don't want to leave our world behind. Ironically, though, the world is what we try to ignore while here, as somehow beneath our interest or understanding, as not spiritual enough. We ravenously study Scripture—and we should—but we haven't the slightest hunger to know more about God's works, only his words are important.

If the Incarnation and Resurrection contradict that attitude, so does Scripture. Genesis 1 and the Psalms show us that there's more to knowing God, and thus more to worship, than an intellectual understanding of God's words. We can't fully worship God when we ignore half of his nature. He creates, he shows imagination; he calls for the same thing in us. Awe, wonder, excitement. When was the last time we felt any of those about our world? Most of the time, we complain. When it snows, we complain. When it rains, we complain. When it's cloudy, we complain. When the leaves blow, we complain. When the sun shines too much, we complain. My mother used to tell me that when I complained about the weather I was complaining about God. Even today when I catch myself doing it, I stop and remember her words; and I feel guilty. I should. We do a lot of complaining about God and not much praising. We don't seem to be good at praise.

Yet praise is what we're called to be. Worship isn't an option. Of all the metaphors we could become, a songbird might be the best. I suspect, though, that the idea of becoming perpetual song in praise of God sounds tedious or boring—that is, if we're honest about it. In fact, the idea of becoming worship doesn't really have much appeal. We're content with Sunday observances.

A Little Polish

The purpose of living with imagination, of changing how you see life, is to become worship, to learn how to worship perpetually with whatever you do or say. Unless worship is the ultimate goal of imaginative living, there is no point to it. It merely becomes another kind of selfishness. We may live a more interesting life, but we've ignored the one who gave us imagination to begin with. The reason to learn more about the earth, about nature, about the human body, about all of God's creation is to instill in us a deep respect and awe for God's bounty, to instill a sense of awe and wonder that we've lost. Familiarity in this case doesn't breed contempt; it breeds amazement.

Just as it is an act of love to discover as many things as we can about a friend or spouse, so it is an act of worship to discover God. Obviously, we can see his reflection in beautiful summer days or a field of springtime daffodils. It is somewhat more difficult to see him in a tornado or a flash flood. It is more difficult still to see him in another person or in a relationship or in a community. That, of course, is where we ought to see him best, since he made us—not trees or cats—in his image, tarnished though it might be because of the fall: tarnished but not destroyed. A little polish might brighten us up a bit, the polish of imagination. As C. S. Lewis put it, we carry with us the weight of glory. Some of us bear it well; others try to rid ourselves of the burden.

Carrying the weight of glory or the stamp of God's imagination may be more of a burden than we would like to think. It makes demands of us. It alone insists on a way of seeing that takes a great deal more commitment and work than shuffling through life with half-closed eyes. God didn't create the world that way; we shouldn't respond that way, either. The diversity of his imaginative expression should call forth in us a diversity of imaginative response. Hymns of praise and prayers of thanksgiving are two ways. But so might be a well-tended garden, a restful house, a well-typed letter, a sensitively handled management problem, a word of encouragement or comfort.

These acts of worship need not be as dramatic as a sunset but at times the affect on another person can be as strong. For two years a set of offices and the people in them suffered with noisy air vents and blasts of alternately cold or hot air. One office had no ventilation at all, but got the noise of the vent right outside the door. Maintenance people told them repeatedly that the problem could not be fixed for less than several thousand dollars. It was like working in a wind tunnel; a telephone conversation was nearly impossible. Finally someone decided to do something about it. It took less than a day and about twenty dollars of material to fix the problem. The offices have ventilation without noise. This was a small thing, but to the people who work there it was a great deal. The workman used his imagination and such simple items as duct tape and insulation to do what a heating expert said couldn't be done. That workman was performing an act of worship and using his imagination.

Twenty dollars and a little imagination. Not a lot to solve the problem of six people—a little more than three dollars a person—except that you can't put a price on imagination. The it-can't-be-dones in this world could do with a little more why-nots but would you rightly call that worship? Service, perhaps, but worship? Jesus said that when we've done something for the lowliest person, then we have served Him. Service and worship are inseparable. Worship is a service of praise and adoration, a recognition of priorities. The acts of worship, whether formal or informal, whether through singing hymns or doing our best, say that we know who is first, who's in charge, who's the boss. This is why we can't relegate worship to a once-a-week habit. We keep wanting to be the boss; our ambitions constantly get in the way. Only by living in worship will we get away from promoting ourselves to head man.

Which is also why it's important to live with imagination to keep our eyes and ears and minds open. God has embedded into our world the hints and images and metaphors and symbols of himself. Unless we attune our imaginations to look for these images and metaphors, we'll miss them. When students first begin to read Shakespeare, they often miss the imagery and therefore the meaning of the plays. Someone needs to point out that when an image recurs in Shakespeare, it's important. He didn't just accidentally or carelessly include eight references to blood, for example. When we read them, we know that blood has great significance in that particular play. This is the business of imagination. Such an image as blood not only has significance beyond Shakespeare; each of us has a response to blood. God is much better at this kind of thing than Shakespeare (it's interesting that blood is one of the images God uses throughout Scripture). He's given us the originals that Shakespeare or other great artists have only copied. Throughout Scripture and in the world, we have the images of God bombarding us, pointing us to Christ, pointing us to humility, pointing us to acknowledge who's in charge. We're either too stupid or too stubborn to see the images, probably a little of both. The only image we're really interested in is the one we see in the mirror. We're interested in getting to know us, not God. We forget what business we're supposed to be in, the business of losing ourselves to find ourselves. The paradoxes in Scripture, which can only be apprehended with our imaginations, are difficult to navigate. We like the latter part of that paradox so much that we skip the first part. That doesn't work, of course. Without both parts of a paradox, held imaginatively as one truth and in tension, neither part means anything. The paradoxes contain some of God's greatest images, Christ being in many ways the ultimate paradox: Messiah, king, common criminal, sinless yet filled with our sin. We can never reach the end. God has made it impossible to pick and choose: We've got to take it all—or take none.

He's built paradoxes into the universe, the way our brain functions, for example, not as activator, as most of us think, but as inhibitor. (Through the inhibiting, of course, we're able to act.) Worship is much like the brain. Worship is more an inhibitor than an activator. Worship is not a motivational seminar or a pep rally, contrary to the practice of many of us. Rather, it inhibits us from getting out of focus. It inhibits us from thinking about ourselves. It inhibits us from the wrong influences. It inhibits our selfishness and pride. Without the inhibiting function of the brain, we would be so bombarded by chemicals, sensations, energy, and stimulation that we would be unable to function; our bodies would close up shop, cells overloaded. The brain is on the job twenty-four hours a day, every day of our lives. Let it lapse and the result is painful and tragic. We should worship as the brain functions. Every aspect of ourselves should thrum with worship, search for ways to express it, learn as much as we can about the works of God to better position our imaginations for worship. Instead we are lax and flabby. We give ourselves a week to slip back into comfortable though harmful habits. We're deeply in debt and a payment once a week with extravagance the other six days ensures that we will never recover. One day of health can never make up for six days of illness.

Many of us are such non-worshiping creatures that it will take some time before we can incarnate worship. Recovering alcoholics or drug addicts tell themselves one thing every day: I can't promise to be drug-free for the rest of my life, but I can promise to be drug-free today. The work of becoming worship must be approached in much the same way with God's anointing help. Even looking a few days ahead will probably get our imaginations sidetracked from today, from now. Today is the only day we can promise to worship.

Chapter 14

Come to the Party

I f worship is to be a constant activity of the Christian as I have suggested, we must learn to juxtapose the seemingly unconnected. It's hard to understand how scrubbing the floor or taking the car to the garage for a tune-up has anything to do with worship, but somehow it does. The reason for worship may be different for each person; I would relate those activities to duty and responsibility and a lowly act of stewardship—caring for what God has given. Someone else might find a different reason to worship God for dirty floors or carburetors. Nothing in life is unimportant as a metaphor for imagination or worship. What is important is looking for them.

Jesus' metaphors, as contrasted with, say, Lewis Thomas's, intend to teach us what life is all about, who he is, what God is like, what the kingdom is all about. Jesus is the connector between physical and spiritual reality. According to his metaphors, spiritual reality is a whole lot more physical than we have ever wanted to admit. It's not hocus-pocus, mumbo-jumbo, which should be our quarrel with cults and the occult. It's not religion with forms and formulas. No abracadabras need apply. It's water, seeds, corn, fruit, wine, bread. This is the stuff we know. It doesn't come in a plain brown wrapper marked *Top Secret* or *Danger! Only initiates dare open*. Anyone can bake bread (and if a few more people did they might find themselves less bored and more in tune with what Jesus meant when he said the kingdom is like leaven; every bread-baker knows once the yeast is in the dough, you can't get it out; every breadbaker, too, at one time or another, has discovered what happens when the yeast is dead before it gets into the dough: a murder mystery could be written with a loaf as the weapon). Anyone can throw a few seeds into the ground and watch them germinate. Anyone can quench his thirst with a tall glass of cool water.

Other people may have the metaphors educated out of them, but Christians have to reassert the ability to find metaphors. Metaphoric aptitude is something we all have and need; we cannot leave it to the experts. Metaphors are part and parcel of our faith. They are the way we know our faith, the way we know God. If we've seen Jesus, we've seen the Father, and Jesus himself tells us that he is understood best as a metaphor. The metaphors already exist; all we need to do is reveal them. Jesus pointed the way, and Paul continued his use of metaphors.

At the same time, we must keep in mind that our metaphors are only an approximation of truth. They point to truth; they help us imaginatively understand the truth; they help us explain the truth to others. Metaphors serve the same function as Jesus' parables did, both to make the truth plain and obscure it simultaneously. Because metaphors are limited, they obscure. They can also be paradoxical or quixotic. But we cannot fall into the trap of thinking the metaphor is the thing itself; it's not. It's merely a pointer, the best pointer available no doubt, but still only a pointer. The fact that our metaphors concern concrete and tangible reality makes it harder at times to remember that metaphors aren't the thing itself. Jesus isn't really water, nor are we literally branches, but the analogies are the closest we can get to what we are. Metaphors we make ourselves—hands, feet, flowers, compost, whatever—will help us define ourselves and focus our faith and purpose. But most of us won't literally become those things. (A person such as Mother Teresa may come close to physically becoming her metaphor.)

The danger of literal thinking is far less than the danger not to think and live metaphorically—to ignore the imagination. If imagination is crucial for the theoretical sciences (or perhaps any science) and for other intellectual endeavors, it is no less essential for the Christian life. The patterns for imaginative living are the same: rest, isolation, image-making, juxtaposing ideas that previously had not been put together. It's another use of our imaginative and physical eyes, a use some of us insist on retaining as we grow up, and a use that others lose. Robert Farrar Capon has said that Christian education should focus on stocking people's imaginations. Right now, the stock is pretty low. We've ignored the metaphoric nature of the Bible, and we haven't spent much time thinking of fresh metaphors. Our worship is bereft and sterile, our path littered with potholes. We need to fill them up with sturdy metaphors and images of our faith. We've been looking too closely and for too long at the periods and commas of Scripture and the Christian life; we have missed the meaning. If we move back a little from the punctuation, we'll see words, then sentences, paragraphs, whole ideas.

The Most Eligible Bachelor

God has given us a vision, a delightful picture of his purpose—a bridegroom coming for his bride, a love song, a love feast. (The problem with interpreting the Song of Solomon as an allegory for Christ and the Church is that we don't take it literally enough.) God courts us patiently and lovingly; he woos us diligently and imaginatively. No lover has ever given his loved one so much beauty. What is a basket of flowers compared to a grove of birches, a stand of pines, a meadow of daisies? God is extravagant in his love; we are parsimonious when we ask to see the contract and check every crossed *t* and dotted *i*. We want to know the terms, the conditions, the rules, the steps. God says never mind all that, just come to the wedding feast; let me look at your loveliness. We want to know what to wear. All of God's "never minds" don't make a dent in our dull, unimaginative minds. It's all too much—feasting, and parties, and spitted veal, succulent lamb. Someone had to do a lot of work to get this party ready. The woods needed to be cleared, tables laid, dishes set out. And besides, what about the bloody work of killing the lamb, spearing the veal, stuffing the pig. "Why," we say horrified, "something had to die." "Right," says God, "someone did. But that too is my business. Just relax and enjoy yourselves. It's not every day you get married to the most eligible bachelor who's ever said 'I do.'"

Even without the metaphors, images, symbols, trappings, colors, textures, shapes, forms—the sheer abundance of sensuality that God gives us—his love would be pretty extravagant. But he has added all the ceremony, all the sights, smells, tastes, textures to help his courting of us, his bride. He enjoys it. What is extravagance to us is the common stuff of his life. He would be untrue to his nature to avoid the luxuries. You see, he remembers Eden. He knows what all this was supposed to be like. The metaphors were supposed to be real and not approximate. Imagination was to be as tangible and tangy as oranges or mangoes. We caused it to rot; and we cannot remember, no matter how many of us have tried—poets, scientists, ordinary creatures. Our memories are as crucial to imagination as are our senses. But memory is limited. Every once in a while we may get a whiff of some nearly primeval memory or a glimpse of what we once had and will again—on the first full spring day abundant with color and shape or the soft first fall of snow—but those are only glimpses, we admit sadly. No doubt they're part of God's courtship; no doubt there is somewhere genetically stored or encoded in our brains a small memory of the original intent (it is really unimportant whether scientists ever discover it; we know it's there because we long to return). God is not a God of either/or but of both/and.

Here it all is. Life replete with metaphors, extravagant with senses-stirring objects. Our lover comes, persistent in his wooing, insinuatingly seductive. What lover doesn't enjoy being loved? What woman isn't excited by the attentions of the one who pursues her? But perhaps that's part of the problem. Jesus, here, has used a metaphor that most men find difficult to understand. A man has no idea how it feels to be wooed, only to woo. This isn't an image that gets emphasized a great deal from pulpits or books of theology. Yet to understand the extravagant imagination of God, all of us must place ourselves in the position of the bride. The heady delight of newly awakened love, the shy but eager acceptance of gifts of love, the straining patience as you wait for your loved one, longing to say yes. To become God's bride, men as as well as women need to know what it means to submit to love's call, to be the pursued, not the pursuer.

Discovering Our Bridegroom

Imagination is not a matter merely of the mind or intellect, of linguistic skills. It encompasses every sense we have. It is as much physical as it is mental. Imagination takes the colors, shapes, textures, and tastes, as well as ideas, and transforms them into images and metaphors that help explain what we're all about. They delight us. God comes to us in these images and metaphors, and he comes in joy and love with an easy yoke and a weightless burden: It is not hard to be married to God.

Provided. There is always a "provided" among us human beings. If anyone is unequally yoked in this marriage, it is God to us, sinful and weak. Yet he unites himself to us willingly with the yoke of Christ. But back to "provided"; provided we practice the principle of imagination that is no less true in our marriage relationship to God than it is to our earthly marriages (or other relationships). Discovery. Always trying to learn something new about our bridegroom. What does he like? What are his preferences? His delights? His hobbies? His thoughts? Ideas? We needn't be physically isolated to focus our imaginative energy on God. Ultimately, God gave us imagination so we could be yoked to him, so we could enjoy him, so we could worship him.

God knew it would be difficult for us once outside the Garden of Eden and inside our sin. (Obviously, it was difficult for us even inside Eden, too difficult, apparently, or we'd still be there.) But he gives us images and metaphors to sustain us now, just as surely as he gave the Israelites the Ark of the Covenant, the clouds and pillars of fire to lead them out of the wilderness, the Promised Land to sustain their imaginations and spirits for generations. During the Babylonian captivity he gave them the remembrance of Jerusalem; "If I forget thee, O Jerusalem" is a poignant hymn of imaginative memory. Serpent, staff, shepherd's crook, sling, tree, cross, loaves and fish, stone: these are the images of God's story; they appeal to our senses and emotions as well as to our intellects. And what a marvelous storyteller God is.

How curious are we about this storyteller? Are we curious about God, or, really—if we were honest—bored by him? Do we see the wonders around us and say, "So what! I don't like science." Or do we try to see inside the wonders from the maker's point of view? Not all of us are Einsteins, Thomas Edisons, or Lewis Thomases. But all of us can read, listen, learn, investigate. All of us can discover discovery. We can fall in love with God. He longs to have us do so and could have made it impossible for us to refuse—he's nearly done so anyway, as irresistible as his love is. No lover wants a forced love, but a spontaneous one. Once we fall in love with God, we'll have an insatiable longing to know what he's done in every way. We cut ourselves off from half of God, at least when we only study Scripture. Granted, we can't learn about every aspect of God's creation—not right away, anyhow. But each of us could pick an area to investigate—the oceans, weather, brain research, cell biology—and dedicate some time to reading what we can find on the subjects.

But science doesn't have to be the only place we study God. We can study him in history, in art, in poetry, in literature, in music. Again let me repeat. I am not recommending this kind of natural study of God over a biblical study of God. It's not a question of either/or but of both/and. We need to broaden our appreciation of God, expand our imaginations, stretch our minds. We need a new way of seeing. The Bible covers the bones of God, and every medical student knows how important it is to learn the bones. But there's more to a body than the bones. Fall in love with God; fall in love with something of his that you know nothing about. Study his shape, his form, his texture. Again, to appreciate his shape and texture, we must understand his bones. No artist can paint the human body until he knows the bones. It's impossible even to paint a face unless the artist can see the skeletal structure underneath the curve of the cheek or the sheen of the skin. The Bible is the skeleton of God; his creation is his flesh and blood.

It may be difficult for us to fall in love with someone's bones, but when we put the whole body together and see its loveliness, then love should come. We don't love God, not in that way. We study him and analyze him and try often to second-guess him, but we don't just love him, revel in his existence, joy in his life. That, of course, is what worship is all about. And that is the purpose for studying what God has done, for apprehending with the senses as well as the intellect, the imagination as well as the mind, the nature of God: to worship him better, and then to love our neighbors, friends, family, acquaintances, world, and ourselves better, too. Jesus talks about entering the kingdom as a child. He's talking about wonder, awe, and the capacity for sheer fun that a child has, not worried about yesterday and no thoughts for tomorrow. The only kind of time is now time, the only event the child's love of play. Children don't analyze what their play means or why colors and textures excite them. They just enjoy them. They exuberantly make metaphors and don't care or know what they've done. Children know only one way to live, and that is imaginatively. Jesus urges us to return to that state.

Becoming What God Intended Us to Be

Brennan Manning, a Catholic priest, learned this lesson from a wise spiritual director at a retreat. Manning had planned a rigorous schedule for himself—five hours of prayer a day, plus intense study shrouded in silence. When he arrived, his spiritual director handed him two things—soap bubbles and a box of crayons. He was told to spend his day blowing bubbles and doodling. Manning didn't like it at first, since it upset all his preconceived notions of what a retreat was for and what spiritual meant. But he did it, and learned something valuable. The spiritual director wanted to teach him what it meant to become a child again. He used a literal, and yet imaginative, way of re-structuring the priest's attitudes. Manning learned what the spiritual director intended him to, the simple yet difficult task of living completely in God's hands, with the trust and love of a child, living now, and not then or once. Perhaps we too, should get out the crayons and shake up soap bubbles.

Louise B. Young in *The Blue Planet* describes a lovely crystal that she bought from a small boy during a trip through the Atlas Mountains: the beauty of the geode, the rock crystal in the light, "the gleaming facets sending rays deep into the purple shadows of the farthest recesses. . . . like a star turned inside out."[1] That's on the inside. But the outside? Nothing too re-markable, just a brown, ordinary rock. "On close inspection I can see that its gnarled exterior is composed largely of small, irregular quartz crystals, the same ingredient that comprises more than 99 percent of the brilliant amethysts inside. When the geode is closed, it is hard to imagine that it contains anything remarkable. The little Berber boys who roam the shaly slopes of the Atlas Mountains must have learned from long experience how to distinguish between an ordinary rock and one that holds a nest of gems inside."[2] Imagination is like that geode, perhaps dull and uninteresting on the surface, but full of the most brilliant gems when you break it open. Yet that crystal could also be an image of ourselves, what God can see when he looks inside, what he wants to reveal to ourselves and to everyone else. The geode has it all—color, shape, texture, light, shadow. It is everything its maker intended. In the image of the geode we and imagination become one.

Yet, words ultimately are insufficient; deeds of the flesh, good or bad, speak more clearly. If words had been sufficient, we would have had no Incarnation, no metaphor made blood and mitochondria, DNA, and corpus callosum. What we make ourselves, the metaphors we become, are far more important than the words we pray or sing or hear. Worshiping God with words only goes so far. Worshiping him with imagination as a child, giving him ourselves—feeble attempts at metaphors, symbols, and images—is to meet him as he met us.

There is so much more to imagination than we can ever grasp, for we can never get to the end of what it means to be made in God's image. Somehow we've got his bones and blood; somehow we've got to show that. We may look as dull on the outside as Louise Young's geode; we may even look and feel that way to ourselves. But let God crack us open with his imagination and see what beauty lies within.

Chapter 14, Notes

1. Louise B. Young, *The Blue Planet* (Boston: Little, Brown & Co., 1984), p. 174.

2. Ibid.

Chapter 15

Thorny Issues Resolved

Actually, the Knight had no idea what to do with the Witch or why he wanted to keep her around. His archenemy volunteers to move, and he talks about giving her a permanent position? He found it hard to believe. The two of them were totally incompatible, as were she and Dendra. Dendrites wanted peace, order, three good meals a day, and a comfortable way to make a living. Sudden twists and turns in life weren't for them. Their language didn't even have a word for *surprise* in it. Yet since the Witch had started bothering them, they'd had quite a few. He knew the two of them couldn't live in the same land together. The Knight was back in his old quandary. He couldn't give her the Kingdom. Look what she'd done with it in just a few days. And he didn't really know how to fight her. She'd just send him somewhere, probably back to that ring. He certainly wasn't the dashing figure he'd tried to act in front of that little boy.

As he was thinking, he stared glumly around him, avoiding the Witch's eye. The land really was in a shocking state. He wondered why she had such luck twisting oak trees and cosmos and corn, yet the weeds seemed to grow thick and straight, unaffected by her spells. The bugs, too, were flourishing. If he weren't so tired and his arm so heavy, he'd have been brushing them off. Just then he shifted position slightly to avoid a horde of midgets.

"That does it!" he shouted. The Witch, who'd been getting even more bored waiting for the Knight to say something, thought he'd finally come to a decision. He had.

"I know this is indelicate of me to ask, but if I bend over will you pull out a rather large thorn that's rammed itself between the hinges of my armor? I can't take it any longer."

And without waiting for a reply, he turned around on all fours and stretched like a cat. The Witch could see quite plainly where the problem lay. She tried a couple of times to pull out the thorn, but she couldn't do it. Without a pair of tweezers there was no way to get a good grip on it. (To tell the truth, her fingers were rather fat—short and stubby. She could never understand why most witches had long bony fingers while hers were so farmerish.) So long as the Knight had his armor on, that thorn was in there to stay.

The impatient Knight asked, "Is it out?" He didn't think so, but he thought he'd ask to make sure. "Couldn't you say a spell and make it disappear?"

"No. You'd just disappear with it. You are attached, after all. That's just the way disappearing spells work. I think you're going to have to take off your armor. What have you got on under there? Anything presentable?"

The Knight thought a minute. He was fully clothed underneath; that was no problem. But he'd been wearing his armor so long that he'd feel uncomfortable without it. His clothes probably smelled, too. He didn't know when he'd last bathed. Of course, with all the unpleasant odors in the air, maybe the Witch wouldn't notice one more. So slowly, piece by piece, off it came.

"Sort of lumpy about the middle, aren't you?" the Witch said when he had finished. "You'd think lugging that heavy suit around would have kept you in better shape. Too many brusseldoodles, I suppose." The Witch was vain about her own muscle tone; it had been the one area she'd been able to leave alone when she had reconstructed herself.

"Look, let's not discuss my fondness for cookies or my waistline. Just get that thorn out."

"All right. Don't get so touchy. Just making an observation. Now bend over. My, that's a nice, fat thorn. Really jammed in there. Looks like it found the softest part . . ."

The Knight gurgled threateningly. The Witch took the thorn and, with the flourish of an Ali Baba, pulled it out. She tore his breeches as she did so, but the Knight didn't care. Just as it came out, he thought, thorns, brambles, bushes, shrubs, flowers, spring and fall borders. Well, why not?

He repeated the question aloud. "Why not?"

"Why not what?"

"Why not make you the kingdom gardener? It would take a lifetime to twist the weeds we have into obedience. You'd probably need stronger spells, in fact. And think of the bugs and slugs and soilborne diseases. Leave the corn alone. Twist a few funguses instead. You wouldn't mind if the results were good instead of bad would you, I mean so long as you weren't bored and you could use your skills?"

The novelty appealed to the Witch. Why, it would make her reputation. For the first time, everyone in Dendra would know what she was. If she got tired of gardening, she could always send the Knight away for a little while. It was a worth a try. Why not? She hadn't wanted to move, anyway.

My brother looked up from the ring just as he heard our mother drive up to the house. He wanted to know what was going to happen next, but his stomach was growling. It must be time for lunch. He looked at me.

"Yes, it's time for lunch. Mother's going to wonder what we've been doing all this time. I don't think we should tell her about our visitor."

"But he nicked the coffee table. She's bound to notice it next time she polishes. Mother'll think I did it. Why should I take the blame for something the Knight did?" my brother said.

"Let's worry about that later. Now, how about some tomato soup with a peanut butter and liverwurst sandwich?"

An Eclectic Reading List

Throughout this book, I have emphasized reading as a good way to begin to educate the imagination. Perhaps this is because I've always been a voracious reader; or because my career is in publishing; or because I'm a writer. Probably all three. What follows is hardly an exhaustive or systematic list of books. To provide that would take a lifetime. Rather it is a list of some of my favorite writers in several fields—science, history, horticulture, children's literature, fiction—plus some suggestions of magazines to read. I have not included those favorites I thought most people would know about—C. S. Lewis, Tolkien, Charles Williams, Solzhenitsyn, Balzac, Henry James, Dickens, Trollope, for example—but rather concentrated on those writers people might not be so familiar with. Nor did I include books I quoted; obviously I want people to read those. Start at the beginning, the middle, or the end. It doesn't matter. Just start. Pick any subject, concentrate on one, or jump from topic to topic. Compare styles, ideas, philosophies. Laugh, cry, marvel at, or argue with the writers. Become their partner. After all, that's what every writer wants—an involved reader.

Edwin Way Teale has written four books on nature, each covering a different season: *North With the Spring* begins the series (published by Dodd, Mead & Company or available in any good public library).

Sigurd Olson may be the most beautiful nature writer of the century. He manages beauty, economy, and philosophy without losing clarity or becoming cloying. A hard combination to beat. His first book, *The Singing Wilderness*, will show what I mean. Don't overlook his autobiography, though, *Open*

Horizons, where he tells of his struggles to become a writer (published by Knopf).

John McPhee may not be the writer Olson is, but his books combine the best of journalism and offbeat subjects. He's written on Alaska, birchbark canoe-building, oranges, and lots more. His books originally appeared as lengthy essays in *The New Yorker* (published by Farrar, Straus, and Giroux).

Chet Raymo, an astronomer, has written several books, though I have read only one, his latest, *The Soul of the Night* (Prentice-Hall). It is a sad, haunting, beautiful book that says much about science, the stars, and imagination.

Noel Perrin teaches English at Dartmouth and works a small farm. His three books on rural living, *First Person Rural* being the first, are entertaining and informative (published by Penguin).

Joan Aiken, daughter of American poet and novelist Conrad Aiken, writes for adults as well as children. I can never decide which category I like better, but all her novels are worth reading. *The Wolves of Willoughby Chase* and its sequels are a good introduction to her wit and style (various publishers).

David Macaulay is not so much a writer as an illustrator and conceiver of books. He illustrated *The Amazing Brain* (Houghton Mifflin and one worth reading), but is best known for his series of architectural books, supposedly for children: *Cathedral*, *Castle*, *City*, *Mill*, among others (also Houghton Mifflin). They are beautiful.

Katherine Paterson, in children's literature, is hard to beat. Whether you start with her historical novels or her contemporary ones, you've got a treat in store. *The Great Gilly Hopkins* and *The Bridge to Terabithia* are probably her best known. I don't think she's written a book that hasn't won an award (various publishers).

Richard Kennedy, though, may have done so in his latest tale. He's written many books, but *Amy's Eyes* (Harper & Row) is destined to become a classic. Not often do you read a book that you know will still be read by your grandchildren and great-grandchildren. *Amy's Eyes* will be.

Barbara Tuchman transformed my view of writers of history. *A Distant Mirror* is her most famous book, but *Stilwell and the American Experience in China* is as fascinating (various publishers).

Barbara Savage wrote only one book, but get it. *Miles From Nowhere: A Round-the-World Bicycle Adventure* (The Mountaineers, Seattle, Washington) is not to be missed.

Katherine White, fiction editor for years at *The New Yorker* and wife of E. B. White (and mother of our next writer), wrote very little. The saucy introduction to *Onward and Upward in the Garden* (Knopf), written by her husband, tells why. This is the only book I know that consists primarily of reviews of gardening catalogs; all originally appeared in *The New Yorker*. I, too, love to read garden catalogs. I commend both White's book and the catalogs she reviews to you (especially that of White Flower Farm, Litchfield, Conneticut). Of course, you should also read her husband's works.

Roger Angell knows baseball. And he knows how to write. *Late Innings* and *Five Seasons* should be on anyone's reading list who loves the game and who loves words.

Donald Hall, before we leave baseball, once taught at the University of Michigan. Now he lives on a farm in New Hampshire, where he writes—mostly poetry. But he's also written *Fathers Playing Catch With Sons* (North Point Press, the same small house that publishes Wendell Berry, another fine writer). Hall slips a few nonbaseball essays in the book—a nod to the fact that there are other things in life than balls and strikes.

P. G. Wodehouse cannot be beat for sheer nonsense. *Uncle Fred in the Springtime* is a personal favorite, though I love his golf stories, and of course, Jeeves and Bertie Wooster. When you're feeling the winter doldrums, head for Wodehouse (various publishers).

Patrick McManus has created a concatenation of colorful characters in his books of fishing, camping, hunting, and general outdoor mayhem. Start with *Never Sniff a Gift Fish* and you won't stop until you've read all four of his books—to yourself and aloud to your family (Holt, Rinehart, and Winston).

Magazines of all kinds are good sources of imagination-stretchers. *The New Yorker*, if you can keep up the pace (it's a weekly), is a good one. My favorite science magazine is *Science*, though *Science Digest*, *Scientific American*, and *Omni* are also good. *Country Journal* is another interesting, small publication. *Field and Stream*, *In Fisherman*, and other outdoor publications feature some fine writing, some of the best around. *Horticulture* is beautiful, as well as well-written. *Pleasures in Cooking*, a Cuisinart publication, is my current favorite food journal. *Business Week* is one of my favorites of any of the twenty-odd magazines we subscribe to. Everyone, even those not in business, is affected by what *Business Week* covers. We're all consumers, after all. I know someone who makes a practice of subscribing to several unusual magazines for a year at a time.

Why not?

Subject Index